W0115455

ROSIE JONES

MOVING ON UP

Illustrated by Hayley Wells

Also by Rosie Jones:

The Amazing Edie Eckhart
(2021)

The Amazing Edie Eckhart: The Big Trip
(2022)

The Amazing Edie Eckhart: The Friend Mission
(World Book Day 2024)

ROSIE JONES

MOVING ON UP

Illustrated by Hayley Wells

BEAT THE BULLIES, MAKE FEARLESS FRIENDSHIPS AND DEAL WITH FUNNY FAILS

wren & rook

First published in Great Britain in 2024 by Wren & Rook

Text copyright © Rosie Jones 2024
Illustrations copyright © Hayley Wells 2024
All rights reserved.

The right of Rosie Jones and Hayley Wells to be identified as the
author and illustrator respectively of this Work has been asserted by
them in accordance with the Copyright, Designs & Patents Act 1988.

ISBN: 978 1 5263 6535 4

1 3 5 7 9 10 8 6 4 2

MIX
Paper | Supporting
responsible forestry
FSC
www.fsc.org
FSC® C104740

Wren & Rook
An imprint of
Hachette Children's Group
Part of Hodder & Stoughton
Carmelite House
50 Victoria Embankment
London EC4Y 0DZ

An Hachette UK Company
www.hachette.co.uk
www.hachettechildrens.co.uk

Printed and bound in Great Britain by Clays Ltd, Elcograf S.p.A.

'Chapter Four: Your Body Might Feel Different' has been reviewed
by Dr Laura Archer.

This book is dedicated to everybody who has ever felt a little bit worried about changing and growing up. Hopefully this book will help you.

CONTENTS

INTRODUCTION

Hello, my name is Rosie Jones.

Technically, I am an adult, but I don't feel like one. I'm addicted to *Candy Crush*, I get way too competitive when I play board games (especially Scrabble) and my favourite evenings are the ones where I curl up on the sofa with a friend and watch a romantic comedy (*Pretty Woman* is my favourite, but I also love *Heartstopper*.)

I don't know everything about life; I don't think anybody does.

But after twelve thousand-*ish* days on the planet (yes, I did use a calculator to work that out because I am not that good at arithmetic), I think I now have a pretty good idea of how life works and how to live each day to its best and its fullest.

So, this book is my attempt to pass on my wisdom to you through stories and things that I've learned along the way. But before we get going, here's a little bit about me.

WHO AM I?

My full name is Rosie Luisa Jones. Luisa is Spanish because my nana (Dad's mum) is Spanish, so we went to Spain in the summer holidays every year to see his family. I also have thick brown hair, dark brown eyes and I tan easily because of my Spanish genes. I can't speak Spanish though, which I'm really sad about. I always say I'm going to learn but I never do. Maybe next year!

11

I am a comedian and a writer (obvs, how else would you be reading this book?) and I live in East London with my friend Laura. We have a cat called Floofy. He is **MASSIVE** and is currently lying on my lap as I type this chapter. He's giving me a look that basically says, *How dare you attempt to work? You should be tickling my belly instead!*

I didn't always live in London – I actually grew up in a place called Bridlington (or 'Brid' as we called it). It's a seaside town on the east coast of England, in Yorkshire. Most of the stories I talk about in this book happened in Brid. I love going back there now, but, if I'm honest, when I lived there I found it quite boring. There wasn't much to do there and I would spend a lot of time daydreaming about one day moving to a big city like London or Manchester.

I have a disability called cerebral palsy, which is a brain condition that affects my speech and my walking. When I was little, it made things harder for me because people would judge me on my disability before getting to know the real me (I talk about my disability and how it made things more difficult for me on page 93).

I am also a gay woman, which is another thing I talk about later in the book (on page 102). It is important for me to mention because it is a big part of who I am. Throughout this book we'll look at the big things that make you, **YOU** too, and how you can discover what makes you happy and confident.

A FEW OTHER THINGS ABOUT ME, SO YOU *REALLY* KNOW WHO YOU'RE TALKING TO ...

13

- I love dungarees. I own more than twenty pairs . . . I know, it's a problem.
- My favourite day is Sunday. I love to go for a walk with my friends and then have a MASSIVE Sunday roast.
- I love reading. All kinds of books. When I was younger, I collected bookmarks.
- Even though I enjoy spending time with my friends and family, I also enjoy spending time on my own. There's nothing I like better than going for a walk, having a nice warm drink and having a big old think.
- My favourite person in the world is my brother Ollie. He's five years younger than me and lives in Canada, so I miss him loads.
- Spring is my favourite time of the year. I especially love the first day of the year when you can go outside without a coat on; I feel so free!

- Like a stereotypical Yorkshire lass, I love a brew. It's got to be Yorkshire Tea, of course, and preferably with a good choccy biscuit.
- I travel a lot for work and love staying in posh hotels, mainly because I like to steal the fancy soap! I always like coming home though, because nothing beats your own bed.
- Ever since I was little I have loved writing quizzes. During lockdown, I hosted a weekly Zoom quiz for all my friends, for over a year. It was so fun.
- It's my dream to one day live in Brighton with two dogs. I've already decided to name them 'Billy' and 'Dolly' after my favourite comedian Billy Connolly and my favourite singer Dolly Parton. I love the seaside and I am obsessed with the idea of growing old by the beach.

How would you describe yourself to somebody who didn't know you?

What are ten fun facts about yourself?

What makes you, you?

WHAT IS THIS BOOK ALL ABOUT?

Whether you have been given this book as a gift or have picked it up yourself because you love the cover (it's awesome, isn't it?!), I really hope you find it useful in some way.

If I am honest, I wish I'd had a book like this when I was growing up. I remember sometimes feeling lonely and confused, and it felt like everything was changing around me all the time. This could be fun and exciting, but it also felt big and scary. I was making new friends, having first crushes and obsessing over popstars (a band called Steps were my favourite). I was meant to do all of this **AND** fit in my homework? How?

If you also feel like this, then don't worry – I have your back! In this book I share my funny tales of when I got these problems right (and a bit wrong). This book is here for you no matter what, and I'm always ready to give you a little helping hand when things feel a bit tough.

16

Oh, I nearly forgot to tell you my favourite part of the book! At the beginning of every chapter, I have included a snack and drink suggestion to enjoy as you read. Now, these are optional, so don't feel like you need to drink and eat **EXACTLY** what I suggest, but I thought it would be a fun little addition.

A book is **SO** much more than words on a page – it's about the experience of reading. Take your time, read wherever you want to and read at your own pace . . . it's not a race.

A list of places you could read this book
(add your own suggestions):

- In bed
- On your favourite chair
- Outside
- At school
- Up a tree
- On the beach
- In the car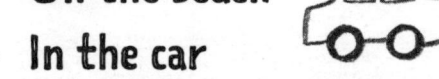
- On the floor with your legs in the air
- Out loud with your friend
- In space!

Okay, the last suggestion was a joke, but if anybody out there **DOES** read this book in space, then let me know (send me a picture!) because that is seriously cool.

Right, I think I've said everything I need to say for now, so let's dive straight in!

CHAPTER ONE

BEING A GOOD FRIEND

PAIRING SNACK

Revels or another packet of assorted chocolates! *Like friends, you'll like some more than others, and that's okay!*

PAIRING DRINK

Orange juice and lemonade *Like a good friendship, they're both very different but it works!*

I SHOULD READ THIS WHEN . . .

I am unsure about a friend or I want to be a better friend.

ROSIE'S RAMBLINGS

My friends are the most important things in my life (apart from my family – Mum, if you're reading this, I love you!) but making and keeping friends can be tricky.

When I first started school I became best friends with a girl in my class, and for years we did everything together. We'd sit together every day, hang out at the weekends and play games in the park. Our favourite game was British Bulldog (a bit like tag, where you have to run from one point to another without getting caught). As we got a bit older, we realised that we didn't have a lot in common. We didn't fall out or argue, we just stopped being friends one day.

Then, when I went to secondary school, I became friends with two girls who had been best friends since primary school. I felt lucky to be their friend and I slowly began to change bits of my personality in the hope they would like me more. For example, they didn't like it when I talked loudly (they said it was 'stupid') so I began to talk quietly, and eventually less and less. **I soon became somebody I didn't recognise**, all because I wanted to please my new friends.

It was only when I realised I was spending more time being who *they* wanted me to be rather than who *I* wanted to be, that I became brave enough to speak up. I then started to make friends with people who liked me for *me* and didn't expect me to change my personality to be their mate.

Do you change your personality when you are around certain friends? Would they still like you if you didn't change?

Over the years, I have made and lost a lot of friends. Sometimes I feel sad about the friendships I've lost and I miss them every day. But with each of these friendships, I found myself wondering whether they liked me for me or for who I was pretending to be? Once I realised they liked me for who I was pretending to be, I knew they weren't being good friends at all.

There are lots of things that make a good friend and sometimes it's a hard thing to be, but here are a few things that I think make a good one.

A good friend should:

- Be the person who is there for you when you're not feeling great. They should offer you support, kind words, listening ears and a warm hug when you need it.

- Be the person who will celebrate with you during the great times. Even if they're jealous that you got a good grade or are going on holiday, they still want to celebrate with you. If you're happy, they're happy.

- Enjoy being in your company. Even If you're not doing anything terribly exciting, just being together is good enough for them.

- Consider your feelings. You can't always do what they want to do.

- Understand that even if you don't talk every day, you can still care about each other.

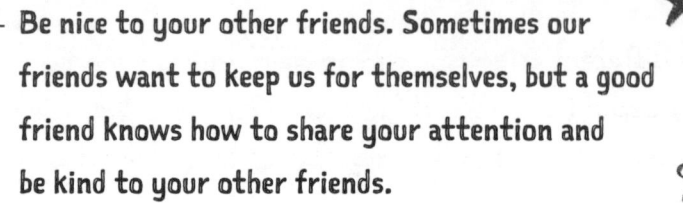

- Be nice to your other friends. Sometimes our friends want to keep us for themselves, but a good friend knows how to share your attention and be kind to your other friends.

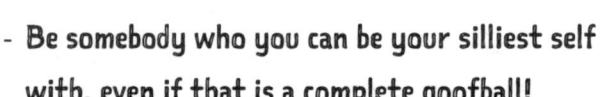

- Be somebody who you can be your silliest self with, even if that is a complete goofball!

Think about what kind of friend you are. Do you do these things for your friends, or do you sometimes forget?

Friendship is a two-way street. We should treat people the way we'd like to be treated. If you find yourself forgetting to do some of these things, then take a moment to think how you could start being a better friend. It's okay if we're not always good friends — everyone makes mistakes — but we should always try our best to be our best.

As I get older, I have fewer friends than I used to, but they all mean so much to me. I try to see them every few weeks, but sometimes because of work or distance, I can only see them a few times a year. We keep in touch, though by calling each other and messaging every few days.

26

I have different friendships with different people, too. Some people I like to talk to every day and others I hardly ever talk to, but when we meet up it feels like we've never been apart.

Here's are some of my friends and the different friendships I have with them.

TIM

WHO IS HE?
I lived with Tim when I first moved to London twelve years ago. He is Australian and now he lives back home in Melbourne.

WHY HE IS MY FRIEND?
Because we have the same sense of humour! Nobody makes me laugh as much as Tim.

HOW OFTEN DO I SEE HIM?
Because I live on the opposite side of the world to Tim, I only see him once every few years when I visit Australia to perform my comedy shows. When I do see him, it feels like nothing has changed. We're still good friends.

WHAT DO I LIKE MOST ABOUT HIM?

Even though we can go months without talking to each other, I know that Tim is always the same, and we know how much we love each other. He's still my funny, silly partner in crime!

SARAH

WHO IS SHE?

Sarah is my friend from school. We have been friends since we were ten, so that means we have known each other for nearly twenty-five years. Boy, that makes me feel old!

WHY SHE IS MY FRIEND?

When we were younger, we became friends because we liked the same music. We liked dancing around the living room together and singing loudly. Now we are friends because we love going to the theatre together and catching up on the old times.

HOW OFTEN DO I SEE HER?

Like me, Sarah now lives in London, so I see her every other week, which makes me very happy. After school, Sarah travelled a lot with work so I didn't see her for

nearly ten years. When we got back in touch, we picked up right where we left off. I am proud to call her my oldest friend.

WHAT DO I LIKE MOST ABOUT HER?

I love how even though we're older and don't dance in the living room together (well, sometimes we do), we are still friends and closer than ever. I hope we sing loudly together even when we're old ladies (and our mums can't tell us off for being too loud any more!).

ASH

WHO ARE THEY?

Ash is my tour manager and I have only known them a few years, but we became close quickly because we are very similar and love to make each other laugh. We are able to balance having fun together with working together.

WHY THEY ARE MY FRIEND

We have similar senses of humour and the same opinions on some of the big, important things. We also both love a good Sunday lunch (Ash makes the best roast gammon).

HOW OFTEN DO I SEE THEM?

If I'm on tour, I see Ash every day. We never run out of things to say to each other, quite the opposite. The more I see Ash, the more I have to tell them. We can talk for hours and hours and hours.

WHAT DO I LIKE MOST ABOUT THEM?

I love how Ash and I can talk about everything. The fun stuff, the silly stuff, the serious stuff and the important stuff. If I ever have a problem, big or small, Ash is there for me. Ash is my rock and the friend I would call if I ever needed help.

I have so many brilliant friends and these are only three of them. Growing up, I thought it was important to have one best friend but as I get older, I realise I'm lucky to have lots of different, interesting friends in my life who all play different roles.

> **What do you like about your friends? What roles do they have in your life?**

MAKING FRIENDS

Making friends can sometimes feel difficult no matter how old you are. *But what if they don't like me?* I always think. *What if they think I'm boring?*

I remember when I first moved to London after university. London is home to nearly nine million people, and I didn't know a single person. **Super scary!** I felt lonely and I didn't know how to make new friends as an adult (I didn't have lots of people around me who were my own age like you do at school). But I met people at work and asked what they did for fun, and I tried to make them laugh (I *love* making people laugh). Before I knew it, I had lots of friends.

Try this joke with your new friends:

I'm friends with twenty-five of the letters in the alphabet. I don't know y.

I have now lived in London for twelve years, and I am pleased to say that most of my friends live near me. My friend Allie even lives on my road, which is great when I run out of milk!

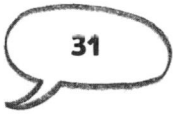

31

TIPS FOR MAKING NEW FRIENDS

- **Be confident.** Say hello to them first and don't be afraid to strike up a conversation.

- **Ask them questions to find out what they're interested in.** It's good to have things in common because that usually means you won't run out of things to talk about.

- **Suggest hanging out at lunchtime or even after school.** By spending time with each other you can figure out if you'll be good friends!

- **Think about what you like and what you're interested in.** Is it a sport, an activity or a hobby? Look into whether there are local classes or clubs you could join. You'll already know you have one thing in common with the friends you make there.

FALLING OUT

Even as adults, people don't really talk about friendships ending. It can be tough and losing a good friend can feel like losing a right arm. But sometimes it's the right thing to do and best for you both to stop being friends. There can be a few different reasons for this. Maybe you don't have a lot in common with each other any more, or maybe it's something more serious. Maybe they're not treating you like a friend should.

Of course, there are many things you can do before you completely stop being friends with someone.

Here are some ways you can help a friendship that isn't feeling quite so good any more ...

1.

Be honest with them. Are they doing and saying a few things that have been upsetting you or making you feel angry? They might not realise they are doing this. Tell them when they upset you so you can talk it through and hopefully they'll stop and you can become good pals again.

2.

Have you been hanging out in big friendship groups, and you miss one particular friend? I sometimes find this happens, so it can be useful to remember to hang out with friends one-on-one. Arrange a day just for the two of you. It will probably be what you both need!

3.

Has something changed in either of your lives that has affected your friendship? Maybe they moved away or have a new friend? Ask them to visit or offer to visit them and meet their new friend. They're probably missing you just as much as you miss them.

If you're still struggling to make your friendship work, then it's okay to take a break and stop talking to them for a bit. This could be just a couple of days or a week. Think about how it feels not to speak to them. Did you miss them or did you feel relieved not to be with them?

If you're feeling relief more than anything, then that could be a sign the friendship isn't working as well as it used to and it might be time to part ways. When you stop being friends with somebody it doesn't mean you have to stop being friends with them *forever*. Maybe you're just in different places right now and will pick up your friendship later down the line. Nothing is set in stone.

Try thinking about why you haven't been getting on so well. Is it because you keep disagreeing? Sometimes it's useful to have friends who have different opinions, because it helps you understand another point of view. Just because you disagree with a few things they say doesn't mean you should stop being friends completely. I have friends who I don't agree with, but as long as we are kind and respectful of each other's beliefs, we won't properly fall out.

A healthy discussion with different opinions is totally different from an argument. Just remember not to be too mean or personal.

YOU'VE GOT A FRIEND IN ME

Having good friends is such an important part of life, and I don't know what I would do without my pals. They cheer me up when I'm down and celebrate with me when I'm happy. I hope I do the same for them.

I think the trick to having a good friend and being a good friend is to ask yourself:

- **Do they care about me and how I'm feeling?**

- **Do I care about them and how they're feeling?**

The obvious way to work this out is to ask your friend how they are feeling. Some people find it hard to communicate through talking, so all you need to do is let them know you are there for them. This could be by messaging them, giving them a big hug or sending them a little note, like this one on the next page:

Dear Allie,

I am so glad we're friends. I love it when we make hot chocolate together, and I love it when we sit on the sofa and we talk for hours and hours. I love you almost as much as I love your dog, Linda!

Lots of love,

Rosie x

ROSIE'S ROUND-UP!

Friends are such an important part of life, and I don't know where or who I would be without my brilliant pals.

My friends lift me up, celebrate me and make me feel less alone in the world. But don't worry if you haven't found your true friends yet — there's plenty of time.

Three cheers for all our buddies!

39

CHAPTER TWO

THE BIG SLEEPOVER

PAIRING SNACK

Pringles or your favourite salty snack

THE ultimate sharing snack. Can your arm reach to the bottom of the tube to get the last of the crisps? One time, I nearly got my hand stuck!

PAIRING DRINK

A fizzy or fruity drink

It could be a healthy fruity one and I will give you extra points if you team this up with an epic burp.

I SHOULD READ THIS WHEN . . .

I am going to a party and I am feeling a little bit worried about it.

ROSIE'S RAMBLINGS

When I was at school, sleepovers were
my favourite thing *ever*. If my mum and
dad had let me, I would've had a sleepover
every day! But unfortunately they always made me
wait for the weekend and the holidays.

Even now, I **LOVE** having a sleepover and my friends
come over all the time for a duvet day, where we watch
films on the sofa and eat loads of snacks.

There are a few secrets to planning (and attending) the
perfect sleepover or party, and I am going to tell you
them all now – you are **WELCOME!**

Who are you inviting?

This is arguably the most
important part of a sleepover
or party – the guest list!

Who are the lucky
people on the list?

43

When I was younger, I thought the sign of a good party was how many people came. The more, the better. For a birthday one year I literally invited the entire class, even though I wasn't really friends with half of them.

I thought that inviting lots of people would mean I was popular and being popular was good. But over time I realised it's not about quantity, it's about quality. It's about inviting good, fun people. And, most importantly, people you enjoy spending time with.

Another thing to think about is whether the people you've invited will get on with each other. Think about their personalities. Do they have things in common? What do you do with each of these friends when you hang out? Are the activities similar? That's a sign they'll get on well. My favourite thing is when two of my friends, who don't know each other, get on. It's like matchmaking for friends!

It's good to have a balance of different personalities, too. You can't have ten very **LOUD** people because that would be hilariously chaotic!

44

Totes awks

While it's important to get your guest list right, it's just as important to be kind and not exclude a friend just because you don't think they're cool enough (or another silly reason).

Honesty is the best policy. If you decide not to invite a friend, tell them that you're arranging a sleepover but you would prefer to hang out with them separately, at another time. If you don't tell them, then they might find out anyway and the secrecy will hurt them even more.

Big group, little group, cardboard box

Even though I have lots of friends and I love being sociable, I often find big social groups overwhelming. I don't know who to talk to and sometimes say weird things when I meet people for the first time because I feel awkward.

I often find I have a better time when I hang out with just one or two friends. It means we can chat properly

45

about things I probably wouldn't talk about with a big group of people. I can be honest with them.

Of course, big parties are fun, too. I love the days where I can dance, dance and dance until it feels like my feet are going to drop off!

Parties are also a good place to meet new people and make friends, which is always very fun!

You're the host, not the leader

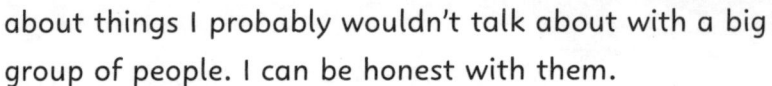

Even if your friends are coming to your house to hang out, it doesn't mean everybody has to live by your rules!

When you're thinking about what to do together, think about what **EVERYONE** would like to do. Is there something fun and different you could all make together? Do you all like the same kind of movies? Find an activity that everyone would enjoy.

When I was at school, we didn't have Netflix, Disney+ or any of the other streaming services. We just had video shops. Me and my two best friends would walk to the

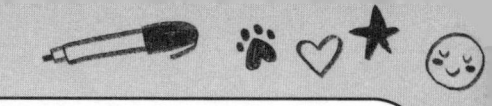

video shop, spend ages choosing a film, then rent it out for the evening. When we **FINALLY** decided on a film, we'd go to one of our houses, dive under our duvets and watch it with a pile of popcorn.

Lights, camera, action!

My friends and I are always creating new ideas for TV shows, and we spend whole weekends together writing, filming and editing the shows. Is there a new comedy, gameshow or quiz show you can create together and then film or play out?

When you are creating a TV show, there are so many different things to think about, such as writing scripts, filming, costume, make-up and acting in front of the camera. Make sure you and your friends choose jobs that are suited to your strengths. Don't forget a runner, too! In my opinion, this is one of the most important jobs when you're making a TV show, because runners make sure that everybody is happy, have everything they need, and are fed and watered. A runner needs to be able to make a cracking cup of tea!

You also need to decide what type of show you are making. Is it a comedy show, a game show, a drama with lots of action or a documentary? My favourite type of show to make when I was younger was a quiz show. I would write out the questions and ask my parents to be contestants.

Once you've filmed your TV show, watch it back! Is it as good as you thought it would be? I'm sure it's brilliant!

Don't worry if you're overwhelmed

Parties and sleepovers are so much fun but they can also feel a bit scary.

If you ever feel overwhelmed and you're not enjoying yourself, then don't be afraid to go home. It's good to step out of your comfort zone every so often, but it's also okay if it feels too much and you need the comfort of home.

Sometimes I go to parties and realise I'm not enjoying myself. It could be because I don't know the other guests very well and find them hard to talk to, or it could be because I'm feeling tired and not very sociable. So I go home and it feels **SO GOOD** to be in my own space and climb into bed!

Don't worry if you don't feel sociable one hundred per cent of the time. Nobody does. It's always useful to spend some time on your own too, because it makes you appreciate it more when you hang out with other people.

Imaginary parties!

I love to plan imaginary parties for when I am older (and super rich!). Why not plan your own imaginary party?

Things to consider for your imaginary party:

- Who are you inviting? Remember, this is *your* party, in *your* imagination, so you can invite ANYBODY. I'm definitely inviting Taylor Swift!
- Where are you having your party? Is it in a castle, on a mountain, on a desert island or somewhere way more cool?

- What music are you playing? Are you going to have a band or a DJ or my favourite . . . KARAOKE!
- What food are you making? Or even better, what restaurant are you ordering food from?
- Do you have a theme? Is it pyjamas or fancy dress? I love fancy dress!
- And the most important question . . . am I invited?

You never know, your imaginary party could give you an idea of things you can do for your next *actual* party.

Parents aren't thaaaat bad

When I went to my friends' houses for sleepovers, I'd sometimes find myself chatting with their parents. It's good to remember that even though they're grown up, parents can be still kinda cool - honest!

50

Even if you don't hang out with them **ALL** night, it still might be quite fun to play a game with them or watch something together. You might all have a great night hanging out!

Don't be lazy – make it!

It's easy to ask your parents to order things online that come straight to your door, but it can be a lot more fun to make things with your friends when they come over.

Make your dinner! How well do you and your mates work together on a task? Together, can you decide what you're making and who is doing what? Maybe one of you doesn't want to cook, so they're in charge of making the table look fantastic. You could even all go grocery shopping together. Can you buy all the ingredients for the cheapest price?

You could try the £1 challenge where you each have to buy toppings for your pizzas for less than £1. Do you think you can do it? If you're cooking up a storm in the kitchen, remember to ask your parents or caregivers for help. We don't want a fiery kitchen sleepover ...!

Birthdays – to party or not to party?

Every year near my birthday (24 June, thanks for asking. I'll be expecting a birthday card from you all!), I start to worry about what I should do.

Sometimes, there seems to be loads of pressure to do something super sociable for your birthday. Often, people expect you to have a party or to at least do *something* for it.

But remember – it's *your* birthday. You should do whatever you want to do. This could be going to the cinema with a group of friends, going for dinner with one friend or just hanging out with your family (which is pretty much what I do every year).

What do you call a party on a farm? A sheepover!

Be aware of everybody else

The best sleepovers happen when everybody is having fun and that's why it's so important to be aware of all your friends and how they're feeling through the night.

Maybe one friend is being more quiet than usual. Without making it too obvious, maybe when you have a moment alone together, ask them if they're okay and if they're having a fun time? They might just feel tired, or they might have something they would like to talk to you about. Either way, it's *always* good to check in on somebody and how they're feeling.

Don't be offended either. They're probably having a good time in your company, but they're not feeling themselves. It's okay to be quiet around your friends but they'll appreciate you checking in.

Snacks are so important – but be careful of the sugar rush!

One time, my mates came to my house for a sleepover. It was super fun and we spent the whole night eating lots of snacks and playing games.

Obviously, I **LOVE** snacks and I got way too excited. My dad made us pizzas and I ate all of mine, *plus* all of my friends' crusts. And I ate nearly a whole tub of strawberry ice cream. We then jumped up and down on my bed. I was so excited that my friends were around,

I started showing off in front of them. I had eaten so much that when we sat down to play a board game . . . I vommed all over the Monopoly board. There was vomit everywhere! Seriously, I spewed all over the board **AND** all of the Monopoly pieces. I filled the top hat to the top! And I've never been able to look at the Scottie dog in the same way. The iron was sliding all over the place! It was totes embarrassing. In the end, my tummy ache was so bad, I had to go straight to bed.

Don't do what I did — stop eating when you're full!

Why not try some healthy treats at your next sleepover too, like yoghurts with fruit toppings and popcorn.

ROSIE'S ROUND-UP!

The most important part of any party
or sleepover is having a fun time. You shouldn't ever
feel like you need to host something just because people
expect it.

Everybody is different, and a party is whatever you want
it to be. The bottom line is: if you're with the right people,
anything you do will be fun!

Stop worrying and just enjoy hanging out!

CHAPTER THREE

FEELING CONFIDENT

PAIRING SNACK
Your choice!
*Be confident, you'll
choose wisely.*

PAIRING DRINK
Your choice again
*You've done this once, so
you know how to do it twice.*

I SHOULD READ THIS WHEN . . .
I'm feeling a bit unsure
or not very confident.

WHAT DO I KNOW ABOUT CONFIDENCE?

When I am not writing fun books like this one, I'm a stand-up comedian. That means I stand in front of hundreds of people every night and tell jokes. If I'm doing my job properly, I make them laugh. It takes a lot of confidence to stand on stage because you have lots of people looking at you. But I don't always feel confident.

Sometimes I worry it'll go wrong and I'll forget what I'm saying or won't make people laugh.

But one of the biggest secrets about confidence is simply believing in yourself. If you believe you can, then you will. That's the biggest thing. Everybody else will simply believe you can do it, and guess what? You can.

Even if it goes wrong, what's the worst that could happen? The world won't end, honestly.

I need a lot of confidence to do the job I do, and that can be difficult if I have a bad day and I'm doubting my ability to make people laugh.

What do you call a person who loves talking to people AND fixing your teeth? A confidentist!

Friends can really help build your confidence, especially if they're good ones. If you're feeling unsure of something, tell them so and ask their advice. Your friends can be your cheerleaders.

Confidence at school

Even though I now feel incredibly confident and I perform comedy on stage every night, I was quite shy at school. I had a few friends and I wanted to fit in, but the last thing I wanted to do was stand out. I also didn't like answering questions in class in case I got them wrong.

A big part of my lack of confidence at school was the people I was hanging out with. Whenever I tried to say something that my friends disagreed with, they would laugh at me and tell me to stop being silly. If I ever wore something that they didn't like (like a new hat or a new jacket), they would say to me, 'Why are you wearing that? You look stupid!' They would gang up against me, and it made me feel incredibly sad and alone. It wasn't a nice feeling at all.

Over time, I became less and less confident in who I was and what I believed in, and I became a person I didn't recognise.

I didn't like who I became.

A million and one ways to be confident

Being confident isn't about being the loudest or funniest person in the room, it's about being *yourself* and caring less about what other people think of you.

Even now that I'm older, I spend so much time worrying about what others think of me, and I always seem to be desperate to make people like me. While it's important to be a good and nice person, you should also have confidence in yourself too.

Some of my favourite people in the world are the ones who aren't the loudest talkers; they are the quietly assured people. The ones who are proud to stand up and be confident in who they truly are.

Not-so-confident memories

Everybody has lacked confidence at least once in their life and that is okay. I want you to think about a time where you haven't felt confident. Why did you feel like that? If you were in that situation again, what could you do to help yourself feel braver?

I recently found myself feeling too shy to stand up for what I believed in. I was having a discussion with an older lady and she said a few things that I definitely didn't agree with. But because she was older, I assumed she had more experience in the world, and therefore I found it very difficult to challenge her on her beliefs.

I'm not saying you should go around starting arguments with older people! But if you find someone is saying something you don't like, or is maybe even hurtful, you can tell them why you disagree. Just be sure not to shout and always be polite. You can disagree with someone and **still be kind**.

I usually try to avoid arguments because they make me feel sad (I don't like to offend people). It's also never a good feeling to have a shouting match with somebody.

I like to keep the peace. So, I didn't confront this older lady as I didn't want her to become angry if I said something she didn't agree with. But, by not being confident to stand up for what I believed in, I compromised myself and felt disappointed.

A few weeks later, I found myself in a similar situation with a man who said a few nasty things that I definitely didn't agree with. I mustered up my courage and told him (politely) that I didn't agree with him. I spoke calmly and coolly, and I'm so glad I stood up for what I believed in.

Having confidence gives you the power to believe in yourself and to stand up for what you think is right.

Trying out a 'different me'

When I was sixteen, I went on holiday with my mum and dad. I was excited, but I was secretly *most* excited to be away from my friends for a bit. On the plane, I decided to be honest and I told my mum that I'd been unhappy and not very confident at school.

She suggested that I spend the next few weeks on holiday being 'the real me', because if the people we met on holiday didn't like me, I'd never have to see them again. Turns out, they loved me! It really gave me the confidence to always be the **real me**.

When I went back to school I felt much more confident to simply be myself, whether my friends liked it or not.

Remember, if you're confident enough to be your true and authentic self, there will be people out there who will like you and respect you for it. If a person doesn't celebrate who you are, maybe they're not worth knowing at all.

Out of your comfort zone

Being confident isn't just about sticking to things you're good at. It's also about exploring and embracing different parts of your personality.

When I was at school, one of my friends was an amazing singer and dancer. She was properly brilliant. One year, she convinced me to take part in a dancing week, which ended with a performance in front of all our family and friends. I was so nervous. This was something I'd never done before.

Was I the best dancer? No. But I enjoyed dancing and that was the most important thing. I tried my best and in the end, I felt totes comfortable in my own skin.

Now I sing and dance at every possible moment because it's something I enjoy doing, and that is the most important thing.

What could you do to push yourself out of your comfort zone?

Is there anything you've always wanted to do but you've never had the confidence to do it?

Maybe it's performing something or maybe it's joining a new club. Whatever it is, back yourself and just do it. What's stopping you?

Confident inspirations

I often find it helpful to think about the confident people in my life, and hope that one day I will be more like them.

The most confident person I know is my brother, Ollie. He is the bravest person I know. He has been travelling around the world for years now, visiting many different countries including Australia, New Zealand, Japan and the USA. He is currently working in a vintage shop in Canada.

Even though I am the performer in the family, Ollie is so much more confident than me. He can walk into a room full of strangers and not feel nervous at all. And when he's travelling around the world, he has the confidence to cope with any problem he faces, no matter how big it is.

I watch how confident Ollie is and it inspires me to travel alone and explore the world more. So I did it! Last year, I went on holiday to Greece on my own. Every time I felt nervous or unsure, I simply thought to myself, *What would Ollie do?* I made lots of friends and felt so proud of myself for doing something so big on my own.

66

Who is the most confident person you know and what makes them confident? Think about how confidently they go about their life and try to channel that confidence next time you're feeling unsure. When in doubt, think, *What would my confident friend do?*

Mirror, mirror

This might sound like an odd thing to do, but it really helps if I'm ever feeling unsure or shy . . . Look at yourself in the mirror and say out loud the things you like about yourself. They could be big important things or they could be small and silly.

For example, these are five things I like about myself:

- I like how I can make people laugh. In my opinion, there's no greater feeling than when you're able to make a person laugh.
- I like how shiny my hair is. Silly I know, but I spend ages washing it and I feel really confident when people compliment me on my shiny locks.

- I like how good I am at buying gifts for people. I put loads of thought into it and listen to them, remembering when they mention a thing they want or need, and then – WHAM! – I surprise them with it for their birthday or Christmas.

- I like how organised I am. I colour-code my calendar and I am never, ever late for a meeting. I think I am reliable and that is always a good thing to be.

- I like how much of a good friend I am. I think about my friends a lot and I always remember to check in on them if they're not feeling good.

By focusing on your strengths and the things you like about yourself, you can hopefully take that self-assurance out into the world. You'll be ready to take on whatever comes your way.

Confident teachers

Teachers are some of the most confident people I have ever met. I should know, my mum and dad were both teachers!

Teachers are able to stand in front of a class every day and talk about a whole load of different things. It takes so much confidence to do that and I think it's impressive.

They have to assure you that they know exactly what they're talking about (and they do), as well as keeping you happy and entertained. It's a really hard job!

Think about your favourite teacher at school. Why do you like them? Would you describe them as confident? If so, what do they that makes you believe they are confident?

The dreaded public speaking

When it comes to public speaking, confidence is so important. And speaking in front of people is something that will probably happen more and more as you get older. Public speaking comes in many different forms, such as giving a speech at a party, giving a presentation at school, or becoming a stand-up comedian!

The secret to being a successful public speaker is simple: *you have to know what you're talking about.* If you don't know about or believe in the things you're saying, how do you expect anybody else to have the confidence in you?

If you want to become a successful public speaker, think about something you care about or want to let people know about. And then perform a speech, a song, a poem or even a quiz in front of your friends and family. You will be nervous at first, but over time these nerves will disappear as you become more and more confident.

ROSIE'S ROUND-UP!

If you can have confidence in yourself and who you are, a lot of things in life will feel much easier. I wish I could get back all the hours I spent worrying about what other people think of me, instead of simply standing up for the things I believe in.

Even now, there are days where I don't have any self-confidence, and I don't feel good enough. For a long time, I didn't feel confident enough to write this book. 'What do I know?' I would say, 'I can't give advice when I don't have all the answers for myself!'

But then it is also confident to acknowledge that you *don't* have all the answers, because nobody does.

Confidence is the ability to make mistakes, own them and learn from them.

Confidence is knowing who you are and not being afraid to show the world.

Confidence is not being afraid to stand up for what you believe in.

With confidence comes power. The power to be *yourself*.

CHAPTER FOUR

YOUR BODY MIGHT FEEL DIFFERENT

PAIRING SNACK

Any box or tub of chocolates

Something with loads of different kinds and flavours. Like bodies, chocolates come in all shapes and sizes.

PAIRING DRINK

A squash or cordial of some kind

Something that changes when added to water.

I SHOULD READ THIS WHEN . . .

My body is changing or I want to know what will happen to my body as I get older.

ROSIE'S RAMBLINGS

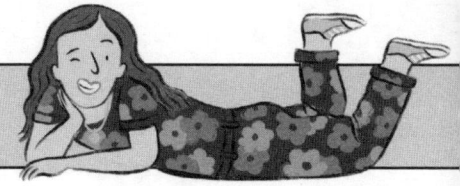

This is a big chapter and I only want you to read it when you feel ready. Growing up can be exciting but also seem scary, and one of the bits that can seem the scariest is how much your body will change. It's part of puberty, which is when your body starts to transform from a child's to an adult's. It can start between the ages of eight and nine but can come later at thirteen or fourteen.

I didn't really like it when my body started growing and changing. It felt like I was becoming an adult too soon.

An important thing to remember is just because your body is changing, and you might look like an adult, you don't need to *feel* like one. Sometimes your body changes sooner than you'd like it to but that's okay. Bodies are just really annoying like that.

Look how far you've come!

Look at a photo of yourself from five years ago. Pick out all the ways you are different. Are you taller now? Is your hair longer? Do you have a bigger smile?

75

Changing can be strange, but mostly, it can be exciting, because a brand-new adventure is on the horizon!

Boobs, boobs, boobs

As you might have guessed, this section is all about boobs, so if you're a boy and don't have boobs, you don't need to read this section, but you might want to know more information about them too. I wont tell anyone if you read on.

Let's be honest, boobs are pretty funny! Especially when you call them 'boobies'. If we were being proper and serious, we'd call them 'breasts' but I feel more comfortable calling them 'boobs'.

When my body was changing, my boobs growing felt like a huge deal, which is why I am including a whole section on it! It made me hold my body differently, and at first they felt odd and strange to me.

Boobs come in all shapes and sizes, and no two are the same. Actually, I'd go one further and say that every single boob is different. One of mine is bigger

than the other one (which is totally normal by the way). When a girl has small boobs, they usually want bigger ones, and when a girl has big boobs, they usually want smaller ones. So, what I'm saying is, nobody wins. There is no such thing as the perfect pair, so if you have boobs, celebrate what you have, no matter how big or small they are.

I loved shopping for my first bra. I went to the shops with my mum and I couldn't quite believe how many different options there were. Padded ones, wired ones, soft ones, all in a million different colours. I was a bit confused but my mum really helped me, and eventually we chose a small black bra. I loved it! After, we went for a hot chocolate nearby (that was my favourite part of the whole shopping trip).

Because of my cerebral palsy, bras were hard to put on at first – they can be quite fiddly. I found the easiest way to put a bra on is to fasten it at the front, and then whizz the fastening round to your back, before putting your arms through the straps. Lastly, I check that my boobs fit comfortably in the cups (I like to call them 'boulder holders'!) and off I go with my day.

These days there are accessible bras with zips or fasteners at the front. Some bras can even be put on over your head. This makes it so much easier for people like me who find it difficult to put a bra on.

Because there are so many different types of bra, they can be confusing. The best way to decide what bra works for you is to try some on in the shops. I hate changing rooms and trying things on, but it's the only way to see what works.

It's important to get your boobs measured at a shop if you can. It's usually free (yippee!) and even though it can feel totes embarrassing to take your top off in front of somebody you don't know, it's so useful to know what size you are. You can keep your top on if you feel too uncomfortable though. I didn't get measured for years, and when I finally did, I found out I'd been wearing a bra that was completely the wrong size – silly billy!

Bras can be very fun, but I still enjoy it when I get to take my bra off at the end of the day. It's nice to be free . . .

Which country makes the most underwear? BRA-zil!

Periods

Before I start this section, I want to talk to the boys. Yes, you! You might be thinking, *Oh good, I can skip this bit because I don't get periods.* **NO**. This chapter is for you too, and you should know what most women and girls around you go through every month.

Periods normally start around the age of twelve, but can start anytime from age eight to fifteen. I won't go into the science of how it works (there are lots of other great books about that written by people much more qualified than me). But essentially it is when the lining of a girl's uterus (that's the organ that sits inside a female pelvis) sheds and a small amount of blood and tissue comes out of the vagina for a few days about once a month. What I'm going to talk about in this section is how periods makes me *feel*.

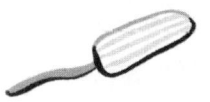

I wasn't ready for my first period at all. I was in Year 8, sitting in a French lesson, and I felt something a bit damp in my knickers. I was sure I hadn't wet myself, so I went to the toilet to check what was happening.

79

When I sat on the toilet, I saw I had blood in my knickers. We had learned about periods at school, so I knew what was happening. After that, even though I was prepared, having periods made me feel very fed up. Even now, when I get my period, I feel very grumpy – mainly because it means I can't wear my favourite knickers in case I get blood on them. But other people have lighter periods, so this doesn't stop them wearing their favourite knickers, and most periods don't stop us from doing our normal everyday activities.

There are lots of different sanitary products to help you absorb the blood, so you don't get it on your knickers all the time. There are pads, tampons, menstrual cups and even these seriously cool new washable period knickers that soak up the period. How awesome is that? If you find it hard to access sanitary products, there are places you can get them for free, like at school by asking the nurse. Or else ask your parent or caregiver to buy them for you.

A bit like bras, these are all worth trying at least once, so you work out which ones are easiest for you to use. I find tampons the best during the day and then I use pads at night.

I often feel a bit ill when I am on my period, especially at the beginning. Some months, my tummy ache is crazy, and I need to lie down and sleep. Don't worry though, all of this is normal and some girls don't get symptoms at all - we're all different. You can help make it feel better with a warm bath, hot water bottles or my favourite remedy when I am on my period – **chocolate!**

Your period also sometimes makes your poo go soft and funny. This happens to lots of my friends who have periods, but I wanted to tell you in this book because nobody told me about the runny poos, and I spent twenty years worrying about it!

My friend Ash also wanted me to mention 'shooty bum pain' here. This is when you get a sudden shooting feeling in your bum when you're on your period. This happens to lots of people and might be linked to why we sometimes have soft poo or diarrhoea during our periods. So now you know! Don't worry. Your body just has lots of different hormones so you might feel strange new sensations, but it will pass. If you are worried about any of the symptoms you have with your period, speak to a trusted adult.

All the boy stuff

I don't have experience of what it's like to be a boy, but I do have a lot of friends who are boys, and I grew up with my brother.

Although you won't get periods, you will still go through puberty and experience changes in your body and you will grow stronger and taller. Your voice will get deeper, you might sweat more, your skin will get oilier and you'll get hairier. This will usually happen between the ages of nine and fourteen.

In my experience, boys also get really hungry as they get older, because growing burns energy. When my brother was a teenager he would eat cereal all day, and one night I caught him eating a big bowl of cereal in the kitchen at 3 a.m.! Just remember not to steal *all* the food from your family.

Hair, hair everywhere

Another big change you might discover as you get older is that hair will start growing under your arms, on your

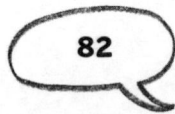

legs and on your private parts. For boys, you might start to discover hair on your face, and a moustache will gradually appear on your upper lip.

All hair is completely normal, and what you decide to do with it is completely up to you. If you like it, keep it. Hair is a natural part of our body, and we grow it to help keep us warm. You should never change anything on your body if you don't want to.

Some adults prefer to take it off, and that's okay too. There are lots of ways to remove hair, including razors, hair removal cream and waxing. You don't need to do any of these if you don't want to, but if you do, ask a trusted adult to help so that you don't hurt yourself.

Feelings

Your body goes through lots of hormonal changes as you get older, and this can affect how you're thinking and feeling. It's good to know this because you will start to have certain feelings and not know why.

When I became a teenager, I started to feel angry at some of my friends and family for no reason at all. I didn't want to talk to them about it either because I felt like I had no excuse to feel that way but really, it was because my hormones were all over the place. This is also a totally normal part of puberty and they will settle down.

Talking about your feelings can be difficult, especially when they're hard to explain to somebody else. But if you can, choose one person to open up to. Even if you just say, 'I'm feeling angry today and I don't know why,' it can help to have somebody there by your side.

I often find it helpful to describe the emotion I am feeling and where I am feeling it.

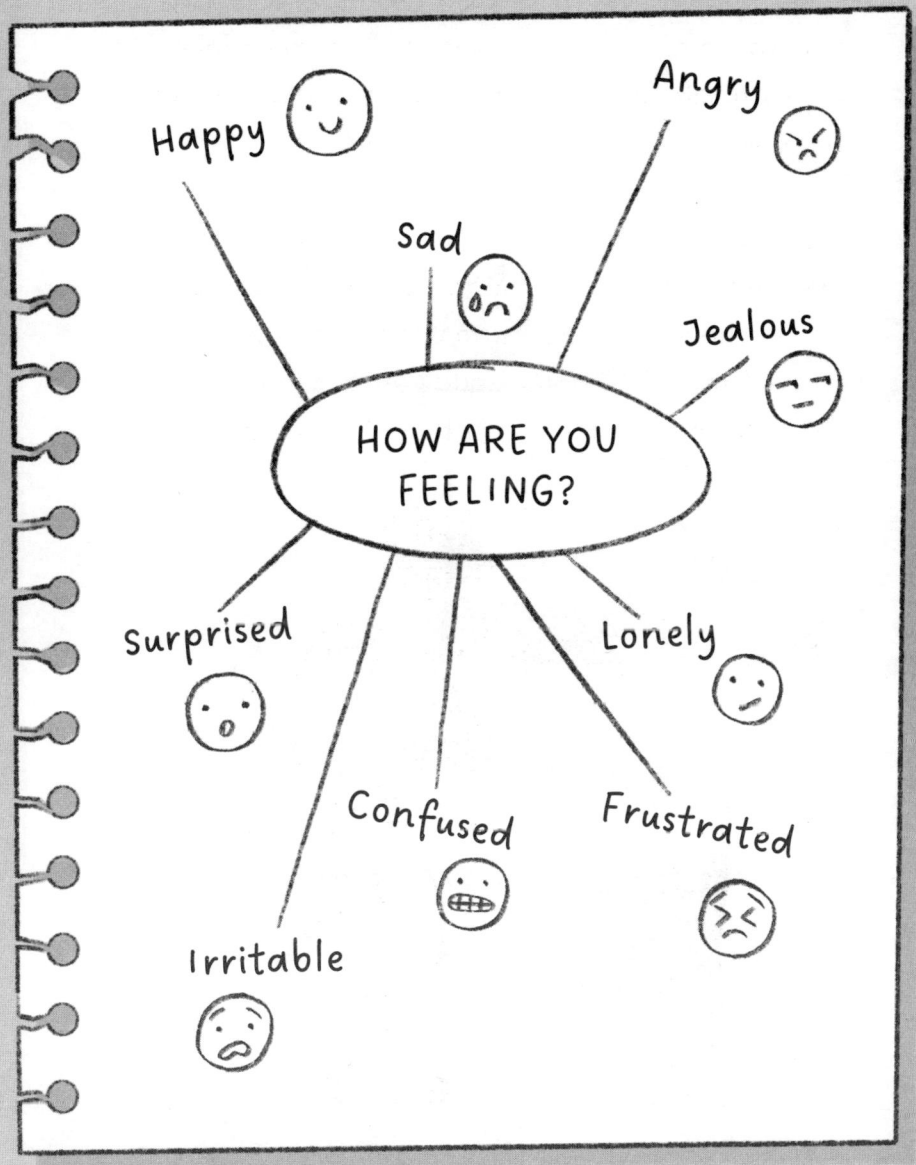

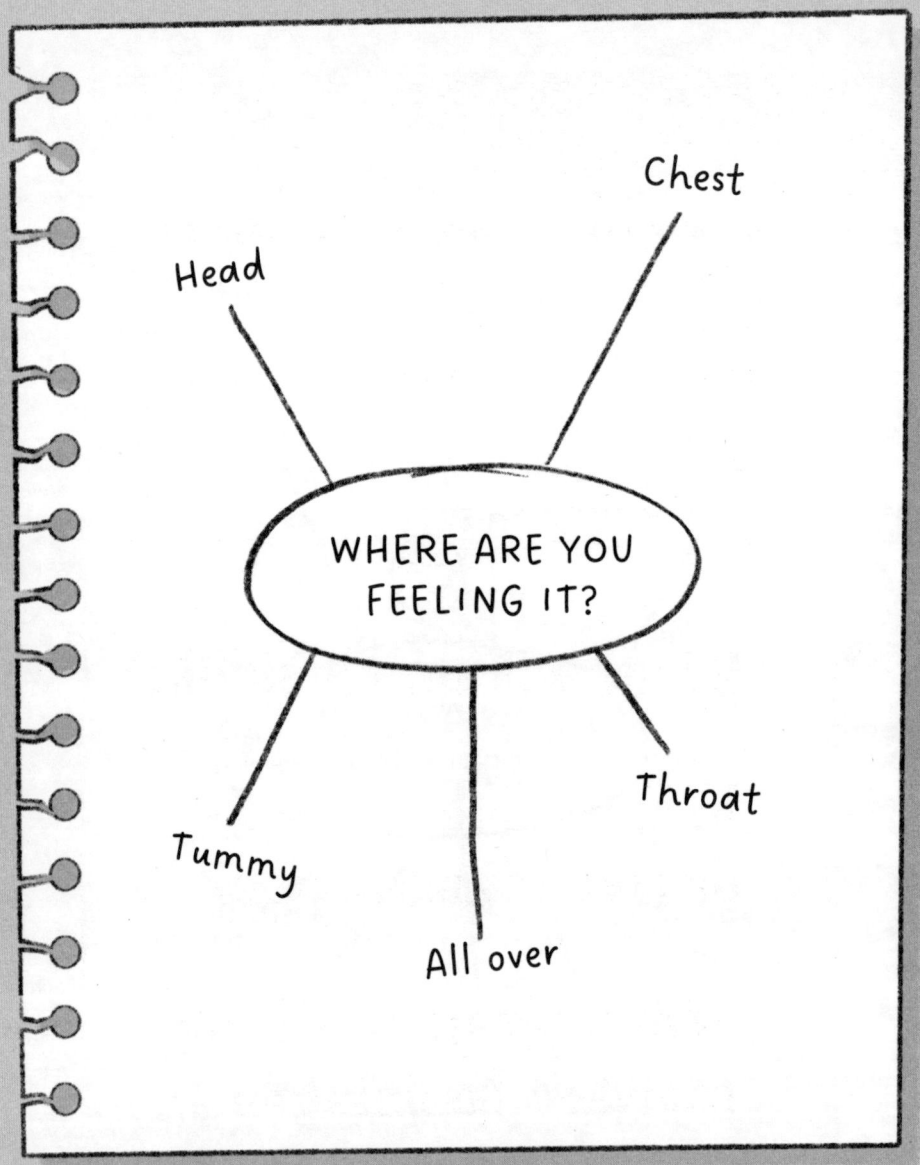

Labelling how I am feeling and where I am feeling it, helps me work out why I am feeling a certain way.

Who will I become?

For me, the hardest part of growing up was the fear I was turning into a person I didn't recognise. It can feel scary. If you feel like this, draw or write about yourself in five years' time. Think about these questions:

- **What will you look like?**

- **What will be different about you?**

- **What are you looking forward to doing?**

You're not alone

Remember, you are definitely not the first person who has ever gotten older, and you certainly won't be the last! A good way to feel less alone during these changes is to talk to your favourite older person about what it's like to get older. Ask them:

- How did they feel about getting older?

- What piece of advice would they give to you?

- What was their favourite part about growing up?

ROSIE'S ROUND-UP!

In the beginning, when I noticed little changes in my body and how I was feeling, I didn't want it to happen. I think it was because it felt like I was becoming a different person; somebody I didn't recognise.

But now I'm more grown up, I know that is not the case at all. I was still the same old me, just a little bit taller with more body hair (and boobs).

I'm not an expert, so I haven't gone into all the details about body changes, but I hope this is a good start, and that you find it helpful. The most important thing to remember it that most of the adults around you have gone through the changes you're thinking and feeling right now (or will be in the future). *You are not alone*, so if you ever feel sad or unsure about anything, don't be afraid to talk to somebody.

Everybody changes, all the time – whether we like it or not!

CHAPTER FIVE

NOT FITTING IN

PAIRING SNACK
Marmite on toast
Marmite isn't for everyone so just sub in your favourite toast topping for a seriously yummy snack!

PAIRING DRINK
Your favourite hot drink
Fruity tea, warm apple juice . . . done however you like it!

I SHOULD READ THIS WHEN . . .
I'm feeling different in some way or I want to know about different people.

ROSIE'S RAMBLINGS

I cannot remember a time in my life when I *didn't* feel different to everybody. I always felt like an outsider and that I didn't fit in. I guess I felt different for a few reasons but it was incredibly lonely at times.

Firstly, I felt different because I have a disability called cerebral palsy. This means I speak slower than the average person, and my balance is affected. Basically, I fall over . . . a lot.

I've had cerebral palsy since I was born. When my mum was giving birth to me, I didn't breathe for seventeen minutes. During that time, the lack of oxygen to my brain meant that parts of it started to shut down. A bit like turning off lights in a house. The part of my brain that controls my muscles shut down and so the rest of my brain has to work twice as hard to compensate for it.

Even though I speak and walk slowly, my disability didn't affect my intelligence. I was always in the top sets at school (apart from maths, which I always found hard) and I also went to university and got a degree in English.

But some people still think, because of my disability, I'm stupid. People talk down to me, patronise me and treat me like a baby. It is *soooo* annoying. I'm not a baby.

Being different at school

When I started school, I was the only disabled person in my class. I stood in front of everybody and made a speech:

Hello. My name is Rosie and I have a disability. I am wobbly but apart from that, I am just like you! Does anybody have any questions?

Even though I was really young, I knew it was important to allow people to ask questions. Some people are scared of difference because it's new and strange to them. But when I explained why I walked and talked differently, they weren't scared any more.

For example, if you haven't met anybody like me before, you may wonder why I speak differently. The difference may seem strange to you and it's okay to ask questions to understand me better.

Ask questions **but** with kindness. Don't just walk up to somebody and say, 'What's wrong with you?' or 'Why are you different?'. Get to know the person and who they are. If you think the person is happy to answer your questions, go ahead. But make sure it feels like a conversation and *not* an interrogation.

After my little speech at school, my class was comfortable around me and my disability. I never felt like 'The Disabled One' or 'The Different One' – I was just Rosie!

Sometimes, because of my disability, I *did* have to do things differently. I couldn't always do what my classmates did in PE, and I often worked from a laptop because I couldn't handwrite. But apart from that, I did pretty much the same things as everybody else.

Sometimes being different can be hard

My disability makes me stand out from the crowd all day, every day. Sometimes it makes things fun. I've always been an attention seeker and I now like standing out from the crowd – always the comedian, making jokes! But sometimes, my disability makes things much harder and incredibly difficult . . . and so painful.

One time, when I was in Year 8 at secondary school, I was knocked over in the school corridor. Because it was so busy, somebody accidentally stepped on my finger, and I heard a big snap. **GROSS!** My finger broke and swelled up. I felt super embarrassed for breaking my finger in front of what felt like the entire school.

At first, I was annoyed at myself. *If I wasn't disabled, I wouldn't have fallen over*, I thought. I now know that this is **RIDICULOUS**. I couldn't help falling over – who can help falling over?! But my difference made me look and *feel* stupid.

But eventually I was able to look on the bright side – breaking my finger meant I got half a day off school (even if it was to go to hospital). **WOO-HOO!**

Find the similarities and celebrate the differences

Imagine if everybody in the world was *exactly the same*. How boring would that be? Everybody would have the same thoughts, the same ideas and the same things to say.

Life is so fun and interesting because everybody has their own story, and their own way of doing things.

I always love it when I meet somebody who has a different story to tell. That's one reason why I moved to

97

London after university. Here there are so many different people from so many different places.

These differences make you who you are, but it's also the similarities that bring you together. Some of my friends are so different to me with different upbringings and opinions on the world, but because we have the same sense of humour, we really get on and have a lot of fun together.

Think about somebody who is very different to you. Write down all the ways you are *not* the same. Now write down all the ways you *are* the same. Does it balance out?

Imagine everyone doing the same thing at the same time. The fart cloud would be enormous!

Is your difference really your superpower?

When I was at school, a lot of teachers and adults would give me compliments and call me 'very special' even though they didn't really know me.

98

Some people even said my disability was my 'superpower', but I didn't really understand what they meant by that. How could falling over and dribbling a little bit be a superpower? That'd be a rubbish superhero, wouldn't it?

To be fair, though, that would be pretty funny!

I know that the people who called me a 'superhero' meant it as a compliment. They saw my difference and admired how I coped at school, but sometimes it didn't feel very flattering.

All I wanted when I was younger was to fit in. I just wanted to be one person in a crowd like everybody else and not stand out. But I couldn't, because every time I walked into a room, people looked at me because of the way I walked and talked. People looked at me because I was different before they even knew who I was.

I don't regret standing up in front of the class when I was four years old and telling my classmates about my cerebral palsy. But, as an adult, I sometimes wonder why it was up to *me* to make sure everybody else felt comfortable around my disability.

Who was there to make sure *I* was comfortable?

Sometimes, being different means you have to explain yourself to other people. But that explanation needs to come from you, in your own time and in your own words.

If somebody asks you a question that you're not comfortable answering, politely say, 'I don't really want to answer that right now.' You don't owe anybody an explanation.

Being described as a superhero when I was younger also put loads of pressure on me to do something really special in life, which felt daunting. I just wanted to be me. Sometimes, unnecessary pressure can make a person feel overwhelmed and not good enough.

So always remember, just because you stand out from the crowd it doesn't mean you have to do something extraordinary. You don't have anything to prove.

Maybe I am different?

Sometimes your difference won't be immediately obvious to you, and will be something you discover about yourself over time.

One thing that could be different is your sexuality. This basically means who you fancy. Some boys fancy girls, some girls

fancy boys, some boys fancy other boys, some girls fancy other girls, some people fancy girls and boys, and some people don't fancy anybody. This is all normal. For more information on confusing crushes and what they mean, turn to page 153.

When I was about seven years old, I started to like a girl in my class as more than just a friend. It felt strange and confusing because I grew up thinking that girls were meant to fancy boys.

I had never met anybody gay before and I wasn't sure if I could talk to anyone about it. It felt like a bad secret.

What made it even more confusing for me was that I was already different because of my disability. How could I be even *more* different to the rest of my class? It felt very unfair.

Realising I was gay and different in yet another way to the rest of my class felt weird. Unlike my disability, nobody could see or hear that I was gay. They would only find out if I told them and I didn't want to tell anybody at school in case I got picked on.

I now love telling people that I am gay. It's part of my personality and I feel comfortable sharing when I fancy somebody. It's not something I'm afraid or ashamed of. Quite the opposite, I am so extremely proud to be a gay woman!

If I had a time machine and could go back to when I was at school, I would tell myself that it's okay and to talk to somebody. So that is what I am telling you now. If you ever feel lost or confused, *talk to somebody.*

Sometimes, even saying a thing out loud makes everything feel better and easier. Talk to somebody you know and trust. This could be a friend, a teacher, a parent or a sibling. I kept things secret for a long time because I was afraid people would make fun of me. But the right person won't laugh at you. They will listen because they care.

Parents are useful . . . sometimes!

Sometimes parents (and adults in general) can be super embarrassing. But believe it or not, a lot of them are actually *quite* useful and very good to talk to.

They won't always know exactly how you feel, but they do care about you. It can be so useful to talk to them. Even if you're not sure why you feel different, it might be helpful to talk to your parents or other members of your family.

I'm really close to my parents, especially my mum. When I decided to tell her I was gay, I was terrified. Even though I knew she would accept me and who I was, I still didn't want it to change how close we were. I also didn't want her to feel like I had been hiding something from her because we never keep secrets from each other.

Even if you feel confident in your differences and who you are, it can still feel a lot to tell somebody you're close to that you feel or think in a different way. If they care about you, they will accept your difference and love you for who you have decided to be.

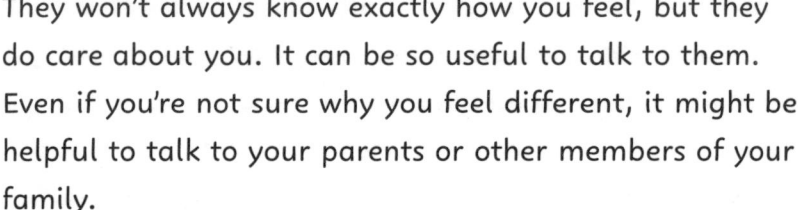

Not everybody responds in the 'perfect' way

If we lived in an ideal world, everybody would be like you and me, and would accept everybody and their

differences. Old, young, gay, straight, man, woman, tall, small, white, black, disabled, non-disabled. We're all people and we can all get on.

But unfortunately, some people are afraid of change and will judge a person on their differences. Sometimes, if you're not like everybody else, a person may even treat you differently, or worse, they might mock you or shut you out because of your difference.

This is *their* problem, not yours. Ignore them and tell a trusted adult if the comments and behaviour become even the slightest bit nasty or hurtful.

But I know this can be much easier to say (or write) than it is to do.

Over the years, people have judged me and treated me in a certain way because of my disability and it often feels overwhelming. But if they do not accept me, including my disability, they're not worth my time or my friendship.

I want to put my energy into getting to know people who accept me for *everything* I am.

Being a good friend

Sometimes you might not be the 'different one' – it could be one of your friends.

If somebody close to you has been honest and shared that they are different, the best thing you can do is listen to them. You could also ask them how they are feeling and what you can do to support them.

Know that just because a person has told you something new about themselves, it doesn't need to change your friendship or what you do together. They are still your friend.

Be a good friend.
Celebrate their difference.

ROSIE'S ROUND-UP!

Even now, having no choice but to be different from the 'norm' can be difficult and lonely at times. I often find myself walking into places where I feel like I have to explain myself and who I am.

But the older I get, the more I realise it's these differences that make me who I am. And I wouldn't have it any other way. I am proud of who I am and I feel incredibly lucky that my friends and family love me and celebrate me for being me.

If you ever feel different from your friends and classmates, try to use these differences positively to stand out from the crowd. Celebrate them and lots of people will love you for being your true and authentic self.

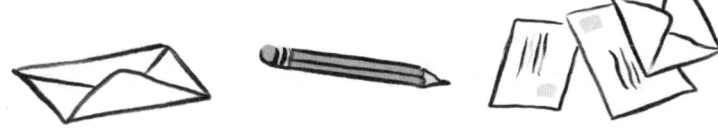

CHAPTER SIX

NEW SCHOOLS

PAIRING SNACK
Cereal
*Even if it isn't morning,
treat yourself!*

PAIRING DRINK
**Your favourite
fruit juice.**
*Apple, orange,
grapefruit . . . there are
so many options!*

I SHOULD READ THIS WHEN . . .
I'm changing schools or moving on
to secondary school.

ROSIE'S RAMBLINGS

Because my family stayed in the same town for twenty years, I never had to move schools during term time. But I do remember feeling really scared when I had to move from primary school to secondary school. It felt incredibly daunting.

I had been in the same primary school since I was four years old. I knew all the teachers, I knew my way around and I really liked being one of the oldest kids in the place. I liked being big!

It felt really weird to go from being one of the biggest people in the school to one of the smallest. My friends and I were going into different classes at secondary school too, which was super scary. I liked my class at primary school! We'd been together since we were four years old. It really felt like the end of an era.

Even though I wasn't looking forward to moving schools, I was able to focus on the positives. I used the change to focus on the new start and I loved the opportunity to make new friends.

Moving from primary school to secondary school

I won't lie to you; this change feels huge. After being at the same school for seven years, it feels scary to move somewhere new.

I was quite lucky and thirty people from my primary school went to the same secondary school as me. But we were still broken up into different classes, and I no longer saw some of my friends all day, every day, like I had in primary school.

Teaching was very different at secondary school too. I pretty much had the same teacher for a whole year at primary school, but at secondary school I had about ten different teachers, one for each subject. Although that felt a bit odd to begin with, I realised it was a big plus. It meant each teacher was passionate about their subject and made lessons really interesting so I didn't get bored.

I had to walk around the school to get to the different classrooms for each of my lessons, which made me feel really cool. And I got my own locker! I decorated it with pictures of my favourite singer (Britney Spears) and kept all my favourite pens in there. And, of course, the most important thing — my sandwiches.

I also liked how grown up I felt when I went to secondary school, which was funny because *technically* I was the smallest person at the school. The teachers give you much more freedom and trust you to find your way around (although I was rubbish at that bit because I can't read maps).

Secondary school was also the place where I really discovered what I was good at and what I enjoyed doing. You learn a lot more, and you study different subjects more in depth than you would at primary school. It was at secondary school where I decided I wanted to be a writer. I really got on with my Year 7 English teacher, Mr Hirst. He actually taught me every year at secondary school until I left when I was eighteen. If you're reading this, hello, Mr Hirst — look at me, I've written a book!

My familiar French teacher

My secondary school experience was an interesting and unique one, specifically because of my French teacher. She was called Mrs Jones and she was also . . . my mum!

As well as being a French teacher, my mum was also an assistant headteacher at the school. Everyone was a bit scared of her and when she shouted you could hear her all over the school.

'I wouldn't like to be having tea at your house,' my friends would say to me when we heard my mum shouting.

I think some people would find it embarrassing to go to school with their mum but I didn't. I found it quite cool. My brother, when he came to the school, even called her 'Mummy' in the corridor, but I didn't go that far.

However, having my mum at school also meant I couldn't get away with a lot, especially when she taught me French. She would tell me off as soon as I started talking, because she knew I was a chatterbox.

But I found my mum teaching at the school to be lovely and familiar. She never treated me differently to the other students, and I felt more confident knowing she was there for me if I needed her.

Having your mum work at the school is unusual but I do think it's important at secondary school to find a teacher that you like and can confide in. Secondary school can feel huge and daunting at times, but it's useful to know you have somebody there to fight your corner.

Where did the teacher take her own children during the summer holidays? Detention!

Changing schools completely

It can feel really lonely moving schools, especially if it's halfway through a school year. It's normal to feel a whole load of different emotions. Sadness for leaving your old school and friends behind; worry for what the new school will be like and whether you'll make new friends; excitement about going somewhere new; and the anticipation of exploring a new place.

It's good to share these feelings with your parents or whoever you are moving with. If you keep the sad feelings to yourself, the problems can feel bigger and bigger, and then they get more difficult to talk about. Don't be afraid to talk to people, because, more often than not, they will understand how you feel.

Sometimes, moving to an unfamiliar place feels odd and scary, but there are advantages too. You never know what new friends you will meet when you are in a new town. Your new BFF could be waiting for you just around the corner!

Moving schools doesn't mean you have to stop being friends with people from your old school, either. There are plenty of ways to communicate with them even if you are moving far away. Some of my best friends live in Australia, which is pretty much as far away as you can get from the UK. But we message each other all the time and sometimes talk on the phone . . . even though, because of the time difference, it is daytime here when it is night-time there.

Remember, if there's somebody new in your class, involve them in conversations by asking them questions. It could be scary for them to start a completely new school where they don't know anybody, so make sure they're happy, comfortable and know their way around the school.

If you really like them, you could ask them if they wanted to hang out at the weekend. Being in a whole new town can feel overwhelming, so you could offer to show them around.

Meeting new people is brilliant and starting a new school is a great way to do this!

Starting school and feeling new

I started my first year of school in the spring term, when I was only four. Where I went to school, people like me who had summer birthdays started reception class later in the year. By this point, most of the kids in my class had already been at school for a term (three months longer than me!) and I was quite intimidated by being the youngest and newest person in my class.

I also had callipers (a plastic brace) on my legs and couldn't walk very well. I felt like everybody was staring at me and wanted to know what was wrong with the new girl with plastic legs.

On the first day I didn't know where anything was, and I got lost when I was trying to find my way to the loo. I nearly wet myself, which is so not a good look! Luckily, a boy called Ben was really helpful and showed me where to find the toilet. By helping me, Ben made me feel welcome. We became best friends from that day on and have stayed friends ever since.

The friendship challenge

If you have recently moved to a new class or school, set yourself a small challenge: try to talk to somebody new in your class every day for a week. That might only be five people, but that's still five more people than at the start of the week! Some attempts might go well and some might not go so well, but you've tried it, so well done you!

Start writing a diary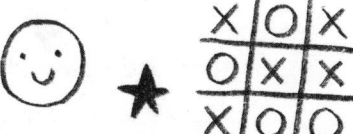

When life feels a bit overwhelming and tricky, I write down what I am feeling. I have always found that writing is the best way to express my emotions. I don't always know what I am going to write until I write it down. Putting words on the page makes everything feel real to me.

I also find it fun to write a diary, especially when you read back the pages, months later. You can see how much you've changed since you first wrote the words and how small that problem became as time passed.

It is also a great distraction technique if you are new to a school and you don't really know anybody. At lunch or at break times, you can write in the diary and not feel bored or left out. Or, once you've made friends, you could invite them to write with you at break times. You could come up with stories together and share your love of writing.

ROSIE'S ROUND-UP!

Some people don't settle into a new school immediately and that is completely fine. It's normal to feel worried in a new place with new people. Be kind to yourself and don't feel bad if you're not best friends with everybody after being there for five minutes.

The most important thing is to keep going to classes, keep talking to people, keep trying to make friends and keep focusing on the positives. It *will* get easier, trust me.

CHAPTER
SEVEN

BEATING
THE
BULLIES

PAIRING SNACK

Jelly Babies! Or some frozen grapes if you want a healthier sweet treat

PAIRING DRINK

Fruity flavoured water

I SHOULD READ THIS WHEN . . .

I feel like I'm being bullied or I'm worried that I am being a bully.

This is a hard chapter to write because being bullied can be the worst feeling in the world. It can often feel incredibly isolating and embarrassing to tell somebody about.

Bullying can sometimes start slowly and it might not even feel like bullying. It could just be a comment every now and then that doesn't make you feel good.

I was bullied a bit because of my disability, especially at primary school. It was usually a comment about how I walked or how I talked. People would shout things at me in the playground and it didn't feel nice at all.

At first, I felt hesitant to tell anybody about it because I didn't want people to think I was being over-sensitive and that I couldn't take a joke. The people who were saying the nasty comments were laughing, so why wasn't I also finding it funny?

But now I know that laughing *at* somebody is incredibly different to laughing *with* somebody. Nothing is ever funny if it means you hurt somebody by saying or doing it. And I should know – I am a comedian, I know what funny is!

Fighting back, your own way

Most of the comments I had at school were predictable and boring and didn't bother me. This was because I knew and I liked who I was. Even from a really young age, I knew I couldn't help having a disability, so if anybody ever had a problem with it, it was on them and nothing to do with me.

But one time a boy told me to 'get some proper legs'. Nobody had ever said that to me before and I kind of admired his originality. It was still a silly thing to say, so I turned to him and said, 'Good idea, do you know where the nearest proper leg shop is?' Weirdly, he didn't!

Why did the boy come out of the shop with only half a leg? It was 50% off!

Sometimes answering back to a nasty comment can be a quick way to stop a bully. In a lot of cases, they're not even saying the comment for you to hear, they're saying it to make one of their friends laugh. By responding to them, you suddenly become a real person, with real feelings.

I know this is a difficult thing to do but try not to respond to their mean comment by saying something that is just as mean.

When somebody hurts me or makes me feel bad about myself, all I want to do is be mean back to them. I want to hurt them as much as they hurt me. But I don't *want* to be a mean person and I don't think you're mean either.

By responding with kindness or humour, you are the better person.

Are you okay?

It's normal to feel angry at the person who is bullying or picking on you. After all, they're hurting you and making you feel sad. But, sometimes, they're acting like a mean person because they are hurting too.

Sometimes bullies are like a very loud, scary dog.

It's very easy to fear the dog. It's loud, frightening and intimidating. But sometimes you need to ask yourself, *why* is the dog barking? The dog wouldn't be barking for no reason. Is the dog in pain or scared of something?

128

Instead of being scared of the person who is picking on you, it could be useful to check if they need your help. If you feel comfortable and confident that it won't put you in danger, why don't you ask them if they are feeling okay? Maybe they're having a hard time and are lashing out at you. Of course, this is never okay, but it might explain why they are being mean.

One time, when I was at secondary school, one of my best friends stopped talking to me. She didn't say anything nasty to me, but I felt upset and wondered why she didn't want to be my friend any more. One day, I decided to be brave and I asked her why she had chosen to stop being my friend.

She immediately started crying and told me that her mum and dad were splitting up. Because she was feeling so sad about what was happening at home, she decided to stop talking to me because talking to me would make everything real.

Sometimes when we are hurting, we push out the people who mean the most to us.

You are never alone

If you're being bullied it can feel really isolating, but please know you're not alone.

Most people in the world will experience bullying at some point. Whether it's the occasional comment or something much bigger, it can feel huge and daunting. You might not know how to stop it or who to confide in, but please remember there are people out there who care about you and how you feel.

You also need to remember that the problem isn't you at all; the problem will always lie with the bully. A happy person *never* bullies.

Am I a bully?

Sometimes you might not even realise you are being a bully. Something that might seem like a joke among friends could be seen as making fun of or bullying by someone else.

Are you talking about somebody in a nasty way and do you regularly make fun of them? **THAT IS BULLYING.**

Sometimes it might feel like fun to mock somebody, especially if you make your other friends laugh in the process. But bonding with somebody at the expense of somebody else is *never* a nice thing to do.

Ask yourself: how would you feel if you heard someone talking about you in the same way you talk about them? If it doesn't feel good, you should stop doing it.

Sometimes, you could be making fun of somebody with a friend because if you didn't, you'd be scared your friend might start making fun of you. You could be protecting yourself. I totally understand why you would do this, but it still isn't a good reason for making fun of somebody else.

Maybe it is time to stand up to your friend. Tell them you don't want to make fun of people any more. If they are a good friend, they will understand and respect your honesty. And if they respond by being nasty and mean, they are not worth your time and energy. Find a person who you can be friends with without making fun of people. Good friendships are built upon kindness and understanding.

Write down how being picked on makes you feel:

- What emotions do you connect with it?

- Have you ever made a person feel like this?

Sometimes, it can feel incredibly difficult to apologise to a person, especially somebody you have hurt for a long time. Where do you start? It can feel nerve-racking to say 'sorry' out loud. It might be easier to write an apology letter. That way, you can take your time and think about exactly what you want to say.

You could write something like this:

Dear (your friend's name)

I am sorry I hurt you. It was never my intention to make you feel sad. I thought it was a joke but now I know that it wasn't funny at all. If I could take back all the things I said and did to you, I would.

I hope you can forgive me one day.

If you ever want to talk about this, I would like to. I care about how you feel.

I hope we can be friends again.

(Your name) x

Remember your brilliance

The worst part about being bullied is that it can make you feel rubbish about yourself. Sometimes it's much easier to believe the negative things people say about you than it is to believe the positive things. If a person gave me ninety-nine compliments and one piece of criticism, I would remember the criticism, because it's easy to focus on negativity. While this is normal, it's never healthy to focus on the negative. If you start believing what the bullies say, the world can start to feel lonely and sad.

You are brilliant. I know this for a fact because everybody is brilliant, in their own unique way.

ROSIE'S ROUND-UP!

Sometimes, if you are having a hard time and are being picked on, it feels difficult to think about a time when this feeling stops. But it will stop.

You will *not* be bullied forever. One day, this hard time will feel like a distant memory. But you might have to be brave and do some things that stop the bullies. Here are a few things you could do to help make things better:

1. Tell somebody

This could be a friend, a teacher, a parent or somebody else you trust. Letting them know you are going through something difficult can help the problem feel smaller and more manageable.

2. Understand why the bully is picking on you

Are they going through something difficult in their own life? Of course, this is never an excuse to make *you* feel rubbish, but it might explain why they are acting this way. It can also help you realise that this is less to do with you and more to do with what is happening to them.

3. Focus on the positives

Who are the people in your life that make you feel good about yourself? While it's easy to get wrapped up in negative thoughts and feelings, this is not healthy for anybody. Ask your friends and family what they like about you and remember those things when you feel sad.

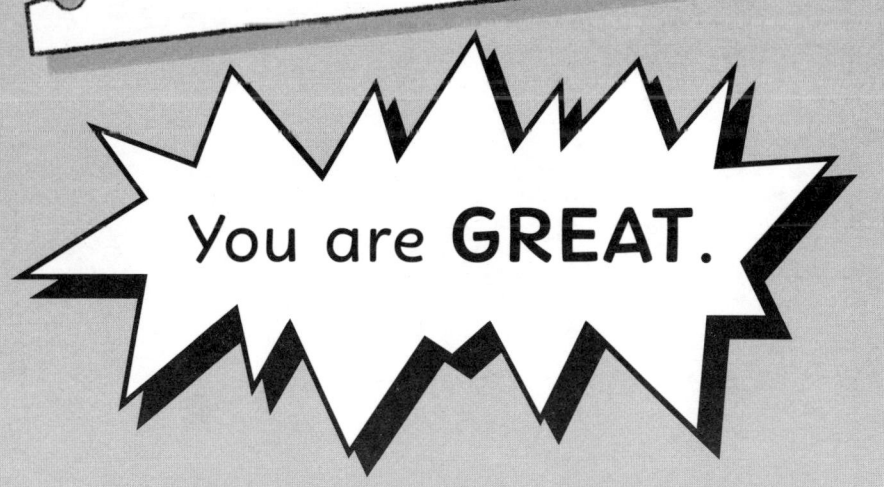

You are **GREAT**.

CHAPTER EIGHT

DON'T FEED THE TROLLS
- they BYTE!

PAIRING SNACK
A really sour sweet or citrusy fruit like an orange
The sourer the better!

PAIRING DRINK
Slushie
I like to mix the colours so that I have a rainbow slushie (and a rainbow tongue!).

I SHOULD READ THIS WHEN . . .
I've started using social media or I'm unsure of how to stay safe online.

Believe it or not, when I went to school, we didn't have **ANY** social media! Yep, that's just how old I am. I didn't have a mobile phone or even a computer until I was seventeen. My parents, my brother and I all shared one computer, so we had to take it in turns if we wanted to use the internet.

When I was a teenager there were a few social media websites, but not ones you would recognise now. Everybody used something called MSN Messenger! This was a programme where I could speak to my friends from school, but compared to all the websites these days, it was incredibly simple and boring.

Facebook was the first proper social media I used and when I first started using it, it felt confusing. Especially when people I didn't know could suddenly talk to me. This was overwhelming and since then social media has only become a bigger and scarier place, which feels quite unmanageable, even to adults.

Hello, stranger

You have to be at least thirteen to use most social media sites and they have this age requirement for a reason – to keep you safe! So, there's no need to hurry to get a social media account, even if people at school say they already have one. It will still be there when you turn thirteen. You're not missing out on anything!

When you are finally old enough to go on social media, there are a few things to keep in mind. Social media makes it easy for you to talk to people you don't know from all around the world. This sounds exciting but it also means you can end up talking to people who aren't very nice.

You should only use social media to keep in touch with people you already know. And, please, *stay safe*. You shouldn't keep things secret from the adults you know and trust, and if anybody online makes you feel unsafe or uncomfortable, stop talking to them and let somebody know straight away.

Don't forget the real world

While social media makes it easy to stay in touch with friends after school and at weekends, when I started using social media, I would spend all my time in my room, on my laptop. (I finally got my own laptop when I was seventeen, so I didn't have to share with my family any more – woo-hoo!)

Because social media was new and fancy to me and my friends back then, we would often spend entire evenings and weekends online, talking to each other.

My mum would ask, 'Why don't you go out with your friends any more?' – it was like she didn't understand how exciting it was to speak to people online.

But now, I understand the importance of having real-life connections and doing things away from my laptop and away from my room. Although social media can be useful when you want to stay in contact with people who live far from you, it can stop you making genuine connections with people in the real world.

If you can, why not meet your friend in person and do a fun activity together. Set yourself a challenge of going somewhere local that you've always wanted to visit. You will then make memories that will feel so much more special than simply staying in your room and writing something on social media.

Say nothing

If you haven't got anything nice to say, then don't say anything at all.

That's one of my favourite quotes and something that I remind myself of nearly every day. I think it's super important to be kind, especially online.

Some people are extremely nasty on social media. The downside of the internet is people can be anonymous. They can say something horrible without anybody knowing who they are.

This can lead to online bullying, which feels horrible and incredibly personal. People think they can be so much more personal than they would ever be in real life.

Because I am on television and people know who I am, I unfortunately get a lot of negativity online. People often tell me they don't like me because of my disability, or they make fun of what I look like and sound like. It's not nice at all. It feels incredibly personal, especially because the comments come directly to me, on my phone. It's almost as if someone is shouting at me through my letterbox to tell me that they don't like me.

I try to ignore the nasty comments but sometimes it is hard to do, especially when the things are so specific and personal.

But I need to remember that if a person is writing something horrible anonymously online, they are probably unhappy with themselves and who they are. A happy person doesn't need to bring somebody else down to make themselves feel better. Ignore them and their words because they don't mean *anything*.

If you ever read something online that's nasty about yourself or somebody you know, you should let a trusted adult know. It doesn't make it okay just because it is online and not in person.

This goes for everything you say online, too! You should never write anything mean about somebody. Before you write anything online, ask yourself two questions:

1. Would I be happy to say this in real life directly to the person?

If the answer is 'no', then you shouldn't be writing it to the person online.

2. Would I be happy if everybody I have ever known read what I'm about to say?

You cannot control who reads what you write online. Even if you are writing something to a person in private, it doesn't necessarily mean that it will stay private. If it's written down, it can be easily shared.

A lot of people use social media to say things they would never say to a person in real life. This often means we stop interacting with people in the real world.

Think about somebody in your life – this could be a friend or a member of your family. If you have something to tell them, and you would normally use your phone to do so, arrange to meet them instead and speak face to face.

I did this recently with my friend Helen. I speak to her nearly every day online but I hadn't seen her in more than a year because she lives on the other side of London from me. I realised that I was being lazy and not a very good friend, so I went to her house. We talked and laughed all night, and ate loads of pizza. Although we had been talking a lot online, we hadn't really been talking about the important things that you only talk about when you are face to face.

Never forget that your friends are proper people in the real world, too!

ROSIE'S ROUND-UP!

A lot of people, including adults, use social media to be a completely different person. This makes it easier for them to be nasty online, and to say things they would never say in real life. This is one of the reasons why you shouldn't be on social media if you are under thirteen.

It's always important to be nice to people, and to remember that you cannot control who reads what you put online.

Be private and take advantage of the lovely parts of social media. Celebrate your wonderful friends and be kind. Always be kind.

CHAPTER NINE

YOUR FIRST CRUSH

PAIRING SNACK
Gummy hearts
Of course!

PAIRING DRINK
Ribena
*Because it's red like love
(okay, it's purple but
close enough).*

I SHOULD READ THIS WHEN . . .
I am starting to have feelings for another
person and I don't know what to do about it.

ROSIE'S RAMBLINGS

A crush happens when you have feelings for someone and you like them as more than just friends. You might think about that person a lot and want to spend a lot of time with them. You might even want to hold their hand and kiss them.

I always had lots of crushes on my friends when I was at school. I would love hanging out with them and then before I knew it, I would be thinking about them all the time. My feelings for friends and people around me would always confuse me, especially because I had feelings for other girls, and I didn't have the words to tell people I was gay.

Crushes can be really confusing too. Sometimes you might have surprising feelings for someone and when you're growing up, it can be tricky to figure out whether it's because you're actually attracted to them or because you just think they're super awesome and want to hang out with them all the time! You don't have to figure things out now. As you get older, you will start to see patterns and figure out whether you fancy girls, boys, both or none! It's not a race so don't stress about it.

I kept my crushes secret because I didn't know what to do with my feelings. Also these emotions felt bad, in some way, and I didn't want to be rejected or laughed at because I liked someone as more than friends.

Share the secret

Having a crush on somebody, but never telling them (or anybody else), felt lonely at times, and if I could go back in time, I would tell my younger self that there was actually nothing wrong with having a crush.

Having feelings for somebody and thinking they are really, really cool is never a bad thing. In my opinion, it's the best compliment ever. If I found out a person had a crush on me, I would be so happy. Even if I didn't like them back in that way, it's always nice to find out that somebody likes you, isn't it?

But sometimes it's difficult to tell a person that you have a crush on them. You might already know that they don't like you back and you want to save yourself from being embarrassed. I get it. I've had crushes in my life that I kept a secret, simply because I knew it would change a friendship or be super awks if I told them.

Even if you decide not to tell your crush you like them, it still might be helpful to tell *somebody* that you have a crush. By sharing your secret, it makes your feelings real. And if you tell somebody, they might give you some great advice on how to move on or whether or not you should tell your crush how you feel.

Are you better friends?

One reason why you might not want to tell your crush that you have feelings for them is because you are really good friends and you are worried about ruining your friendship. I totally get that.

A few years ago, I had a *huge* crush on one of my friends. I couldn't stop thinking about her and I secretly hoped that one day we could be girlfriends.

We hung out all the time and when we were together, we would talk for ages. I wasn't sure whether she liked me back, or whether she just liked me as a friend. We were such good friends, I didn't like having this secret from her, so after a few months I decided to tell her I had feelings for her.

I thought for ages about how I should tell her. It felt too daunting to tell her in person, so I decided to write her a letter. I found it easier to explain how I was feeling in writing.

I told her I really liked her, and thought she was wonderful, kind, funny and beautiful. And that I liked her as more than just a friend. I told her that it was okay if she didn't feel the same but I just really wanted to tell her that she made me feel happy.

My friend responded a few days later and told me she only saw me as a friend. Even though I was gutted, she was very, very kind and told me that she really valued our friendship.

I never wanted how I felt to stop us being friends and luckily, telling her was super helpful. It validated my feelings, and I felt able to move on and put my crush to one side.

Now, a few years later, we are closer than ever, and I no longer have a crush on her. I am so happy I told her about my feelings, because it meant I knew exactly how she felt about me too. I was able to move on without always wondering whether or not she liked me back.

Do something with your feelings

Sometimes you might not want to tell your crush that you have feelings for them and that is okay too. It might not feel appropriate, especially if you have a crush on somebody older than you.

When I have a crush and I don't want to tell anybody, I sometimes find it useful to write a poem or a short story about it. This helps make my feelings seem real and worthwhile, and not like they're just going to waste.

I also sometimes write the person a letter. Even if I don't show anybody the letter, it makes me feel better to turn my unsaid feelings into words on paper.

Writing letters or poems might not be your thing, but there are many other ways to turn your thoughts and feelings into something more real. You could write a song, paint or even create a dance about them.

Secret Valentine's

Sometimes at school if I had a secret crush but didn't want to tell them, I did still want them to know that somebody out there was thinking about them.

One time, when I was in Year 8, I had a crush on somebody in my year but I was too scared to tell them. On Valentine's Day, I decided to put a heart-shaped sticky note on their wheelie bin! I didn't even write anything on the note, and I still don't know whether they got it or if they knew who it was from. In reality, I bet it just blew off the bin as soon as I walked away, but I like to think they got it and knew somebody was thinking about them.

Sometimes, having feelings for somebody might not even mean you want to be with them or that you need them to know how you feel. Sometimes it's just enough that they know that somebody out there thinks they're brilliant.

What did the Post-it note say to the other Post-it note? You're STUCK with me!

Songs say it better

If I have feelings for somebody, I often listen to a lot of love songs, singing along at the top of my voice. Songs are so much better at describing feelings and it often feels quite reassuring to know that millions of people have felt love and had crushes. It makes you feel less lonely and reminds you that you won't feel this way forever.

When I was younger, I would create 'mix tapes' where I would put a load of songs together that reminded us of a person, and then I would give the tape or CD to that person.

159

Why don't you make a 'modern mix tape' and create a playlist for your crush? Choose songs that remind you of that person. You don't have to give the playlist to the person but you might enjoy listening to the songs and thinking about your crush.

Somebody has a crush on YOU!

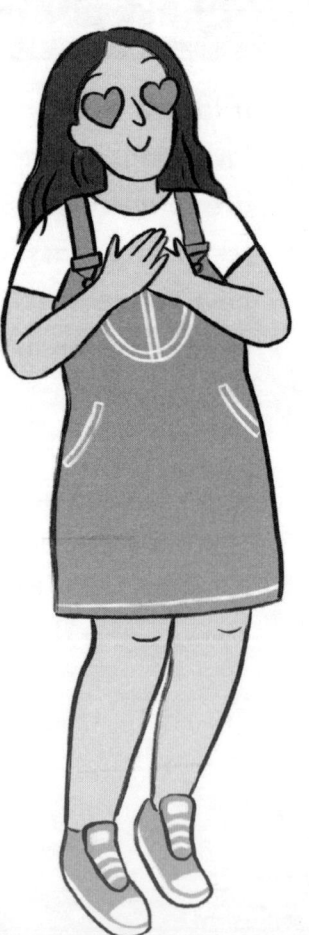

Sometimes it's the other way round and somebody might reveal that they have feelings for you. Whoever they are, you should recognise the fact they have been brave enough to tell you how they feel.

If you also have feelings for them, then great! You both feel the same way – woo-hoo! You can choose to start spending time together, or, for now, it's just nice to know you both like each other.

If you don't like them in the same way, then that's okay too. You can't help how you feel, and you can't force yourself to like somebody if you don't have those emotions. But remember, like a lot of things in life, it's important to be kind and think about their feelings.

You should never make fun of them or gossip about them at school, but simply let them know that while you are flattered, unfortunately you don't feel the same way.

It should never feel bad for a person to tell you they have a crush on you. It means they think you are brilliant. So, whether or not you feel the same way, always be kind to them.

ROSIE'S ROUND-UP!

Sometimes, when I've had a crush, it feels like I've liked them for years and that I am going to like them forever. But *every single time*, I am able to move on from my feelings.

What I am trying to say is, if you ever have feelings for a person who doesn't like you back and it makes you feel stuck, don't worry. Feeling stuck *will* disappear eventually.

If you think it's a good idea to move on and stop having feelings for the person, there are things you can do to make it easier:

- The easiest solution (although it might not feel easy at the time) is to stop talking to them for a bit. If you are still talking and hanging out with them every day, it can be hard to move on. Having a bit of distance for a few weeks or months can make things feel easier.

- Let them know how you feel. If they are kind, they will respond to you in a thoughtful way, even if they don't have feelings for you. By telling them, you will be able to move on from them if they don't feel the same way. Whether they like you or not, at least you now have an answer for sure.

- Put your thoughts and energy into something new and different. If I want to stop thinking about a crush, I will focus on my writing and stop myself from messaging them all day, every day. If my mind is focused on something else, I find it easier to get over a big crush.

CHAPTER TEN

WHO I AM

PAIRING SNACK
Salt and sweet popcorn

PAIRING DRINK
Milkshake!

I SHOULD READ THIS WHEN . . .
I sometimes think I am different at school to when I am at home.

ROSIE'S RAMBLINGS

When I compare who I was at school to who I was at home, I was always two completely different people. I was really quiet at school, but not so much at home with my parents and brother. At home, I was always the loud person with the loud laugh. I felt a bit weird about being two different people and I didn't quite know why I acted so differently at school.

Looking back now, I think I felt most like myself when I was at home. There wasn't the pressure of feeling like I had to fit in with my friends. At home, I could be myself one hundred per cent, because my parents and my brother would love me and accept me no matter what.

Even now, I feel like I change and adapt my personality depending on who I'm with and what I'm doing. For example, if I'm having a work meeting, I will be a lot more sensible and serious than when I'm hanging out with my friends, when I can be more silly.

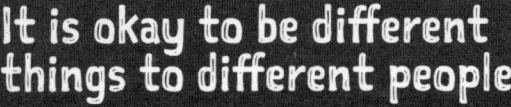

It is okay to be different things to different people

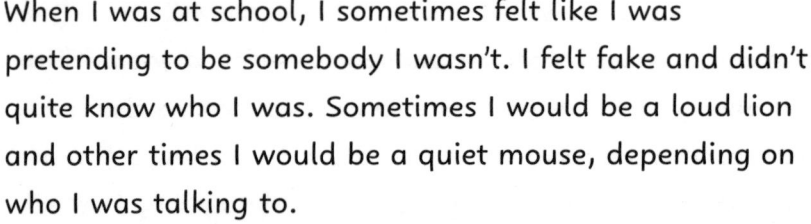

When I was at school, I sometimes felt like I was pretending to be somebody I wasn't. I felt fake and didn't quite know who I was. Sometimes I would be a loud lion and other times I would be a quiet mouse, depending on who I was talking to.

Over time, I've realised that it's absolutely okay to be two (or even three!) different people when hanging out with different groups of friends or family members. You are not being false or fake, you are simply using different sides of your personality with different people.

It is what makes things interesting.

Think about what kind of person you are around certain people. Do you change and do you feel different when you're with them? If the answer is 'yes', then good! It is so normal to change who you are.

If the answer is 'no', can you pick out the group that makes you turn into a version of yourself that you don't

particularly like or feel uncomfortable with? Are you trying to fit in with somebody and become somebody you are not?

It is completely fine to be loads of versions of yourself to different people, as long as every version is one that feels truly and authentically *you*.

A totes awks tea

One night, when I was at secondary school, my friends came over for tea. When I was with this particular group, I was always fairly quiet, mainly because I enjoyed listening to them. Looking back now, though, I think I was desperate for them to like me. I never wanted to be too loud around them in case they didn't like it and made fun of me for being the noisy one.

As the tea went on, my parents were a bit weirded out because I wasn't talking or making the usual jokes. I would normally be the one taking charge of the conversation, but I didn't do that this time because I wanted to make my friends happy.

Eventually, my mum acknowledged the weirdness and asked me whether everything was okay because I was usually a lot more talkative. It was a bit awkward because everybody thought I was lying to everyone, until I explained that I could be two different people at the same time.

Think about what would happen if you were in a similar situation. Do your friends see you in a different way to how your family see you? A good way to find out is to ask your friends to describe you in three words. And then ask your family to describe you in three words.

What did Rosie 1 say to Rosie 2? Stop copying me!

- Have both groups described you using similar words or are they completely different?

- Which list do you prefer and why?

- Which feels most like 'you'?

Why are you different at school?

Imagine if you were the same person at school as you are when you're at home.

- Would that be a good thing or would that be a bad thing?

- Is there something (or someone) stopping you from being the same person?

Sometimes it's useful to recognise why you are different versions of yourself in different situations. Is it because you are keen to fit in or is it because you are afraid of being yourself?

When I was older, I realised I wasn't being myself at school because I didn't want anybody to laugh at me or think I was too loud.

While it's completely normal to adapt who you are depending on where you are and who you are talking to, I think it's super important to make sure you're not changing yourself so that other people like you. If this is the case, try being your true self, no matter what environment you find yourself in.

Life is too short to spend it pleasing other people.

If your friends and family are kind, they will love you no matter who you decide to be, and — in my case — no matter how loud your laugh is!

ROSIE'S ROUND-UP!

Sometimes you can be very aware of how your school personality is very different to your home personality. You could be adapting yourself because you feel like your friends or family would be angry or upset if you acted in a particular way.

When I was at school, I sometimes worried that my personality was too loud or in your face, especially when I was just starting secondary school. I didn't want people thinking I was too loud or overpowering. That's the main reason I decided to be quieter at school. I didn't want to be known as the joker of the class. It would make the centre of attention and I worried that would make me easier to pick on.

But as I grew up, I finally felt comfortable being my true self, because I valued who I was and was incredibly proud of who I had grown up to be. This power allowed me to be as loud as I wanted. And what makes everything brilliant is that I have become a comedian, so I have literally made a career out of being loud and in your face! Get in!

It's extremely hard to pretend you're a person that you're not, but sometimes it's necessary, especially if you think your true self would change things too much for you.

As long as you're aware of how your personality changes, and that you are doing it to protect yourself from negativity, then it's understandable.

I hope that one day you feel comfortable and confident enough to be your true self in all parts of your world, but until then, trust your judgement and be kind to yourself.

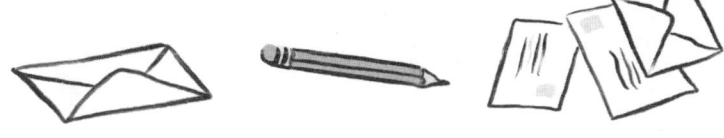

CHAPTER
ELEVEN

BEING A
BRILLIANT
FAMILY
MEMBER

PAIRING SNACK
Marshmallows

PAIRING DRINK
Hot chocolate
*Comforting and cosy
(and the marshmallows
can go on top).*

I SHOULD READ THIS WHEN . . .
Something at home is changing a bit
or I am worried about family life.

ROSIE'S RAMBLINGS

I was really close to my family growing up. It was just me, my brother, my mum and my dad. The fantastic four!

My brother is five years younger than me, so I always wanted to be a good role model for him, especially when he was really little. I was so excited to be a big sister. I remember the day he was born. My nana and grandad took me to the hospital to meet him and I had never ever been so excited.

My parents let me hold him and I remember thinking he was so tiny, which is funny because looking back now, I was small too.

'Hello, Oliver,' I whispered, 'My name is Rosie and I'm your older sister. I'm going to look after you.'

That was nearly thirty years ago now, and I think I have stuck to my word! I still look after him even though he is now a fully grown adult and is a lot taller than me. In my mind, he is still my baby brother.

I felt very lucky to have my family and we are still really close, even though my brother and I no longer live at home.

When I still lived at home, my favourite time to hang out with my family was at mealtimes, especially Friday nights where we'd usually have a 'picky tea'. This was when my parents wouldn't cook and instead we'd have loads of different breads, cheeses, hams and crisps. I would always make a massive crisp sandwich and add a few anchovies too. I know, I am quite weird.

During our picky tea, the four of us would talk about our days and we would plan what we were going to do at the weekend.

Even now, when I go home to visit my parents, my favourite thing to do with them is to sit round the kitchen table, eat lots of food and talk for hours and hours and hours.

A picky tea is when you can pick anything and eat it, apart from your nose!

Parents are okay, I guess

Let's be honest, sometimes parents or caregivers can be legit embarrassing. Sometimes, my dad says the most silly things and I wish the world would swallow me whole.

But your adults are *your* adults and they love you.

Sometimes, especially when I was a teenager, I would much prefer hanging out with my friends. But as I've become older, I realise I have so much in common with my parents, and that I'm happiest when I'm with them, at our house, in my pyjamas!

Don't forget how brilliant your adults are — they made you or chose to care for you after all, and you must get your brilliance from somewhere. Make time to do things with them when you're not at school. It's easy to take them for granted — I do it too with my parents and I am an adult! It's always good to remember how much they do for you.

Think about the last time you did something as a family. What did you do? Think of a great day out you could do together. Here are a few ideas to help you get thinking . . .

- Go on an epic walk or bike ride together. Explore the countryside or if you live near the seaside, walk along the coast and paddle your feet in the sea. Even if it's cold!

- If the weather isn't very good, stay inside and build a den that can fit your entire family. Use ALL the blankets and duvets in the house (the grown-ups will love you if you promise to tidy it all up when you're done!). When you've built your den, watch a film in it and eat your favourite snacks. Nothing beats a cosy film night!

- Why not host a night of entertainment for your adults? I used to love doing this when I was at school. This could be something like a quiz night, a talent show or a singing recital. You could ask your parents to join in with you or you can perform to them. Have fun! I wish I could see what you come up with!

Is somebody in your family being really annoying? Then tell them!

Being a brilliant family member all of the time can be really hard. No matter how much you love and care about your family, you still have to live with them and see them every day. Sometimes, when I lived at home with my parents, I would dream about a time when I didn't have to live with them and could be completely independent. Ironically, now that I'm an adult, living hundreds of miles away, I really miss them.

It's completely normal to be irritated by a family member and they probably get irritated by you too. Nobody's perfect. My brother used to annoy so much when we were growing up and sometimes I wished he would be abducted by aliens so I could have our parents to myself. But living together as a family is all about communication and understanding each other.

If somebody in your family is annoying you, tell them calmly and try to work out a way in which you can all live together without standing on each other's toes. They might just need some space.

Remember, if something gets too much and you have a little argument or problem with a sibling or a parent, it's always useful to take a breather, leave the situation and start again in an hour. When you come back together you will probably find the thing that you were getting annoyed at now feels small and unimportant, making it easier for you both to move past.

Try to see the situation from the other person's point of view and understand that living with lots of people is hard, even if you really love them. If you listen to them and work out a way in which you can all live together happily, then your family will make for a winning and successful team.

Sometimes, it's good to remember all the ways in which your family is great. It's easy to get wrapped up in the negative things, but try to focus on all things **POSITIVE**.

Grab a piece of paper and list your family members (drawing a fun little picture of them if you like!) and write something about what makes them great.

Here's my list:

MUM

My mum is brilliant at knowing exactly how I feel. Sometimes I think she knows me more than I know myself. She's the best at cheering me up and celebrating when I do something good. She is my greatest cheerleader.

DAD

My dad and I have one massive thing in common . . . FOOD! He is the best person at picking restaurants and some of my favourite memories are from when he and I go for a day out together to eat something tasty!

OLIVER

My brother, Oliver ('Ollie' for short), is the silliest person in the world and is the only person who can make me laugh until I cry. I love his sense of adventure and how he loves to explore the world. He is my favourite person.

A big change in your family

Sometimes, if big things happen at home, your family life will change. Maybe your parents will decide to separate or perhaps one of your parents might meet a new partner. Maybe the new partner has children too and suddenly you all have to live together.

Having a change in your family could also mean you have to move house or somebody else moves into your house, so the living situation will be new. It's normal to find this change odd and a bit stressful.

But like everything at home and in life, it's important to let your parents know how you are feeling. Although your parents are the adults and they make the big decisions, you should always have a conversation with them before a major change happens. This way they will know how you're feeling and you can talk it through. It will be harder to adapt to the change if you wait until it's already happened (and your parent or guardian only knows how you feel about it afterwards).

If you ever feel worried or sad about something that has happened at home and you feel like you cannot talk to your parents about it, then you can always talk to other brilliant people in your life. Maybe there is a teacher who you really get on with or one of your friends' parents seem like they are a good listener.

Telling somebody you are not happy can feel daunting but I always find it's really helpful to get advice from somebody else.

Don't keep your problems a secret from the world.

Sibling rivalry

If you have a brother or a sister (or two, or three, or four or eight!), it's likely that you argue with them, maybe every day.

Even though my brother and I always got on and loved to play together, we would still argue and bicker, even about the smallest things. Usually, it was about who was holding the remote control for the television and therefore who was in charge of picking which television programme we watched.

We would also wrestle each other and play-fight, until he got much bigger and stronger than me. One day, we were play-fighting in the living room and I accidentally scratched a lot of paint off the wall. I knew I had done it but because I didn't want to confess, I blamed my brother. Because I was the older sister and never usually lied, my mum and dad believed me and he got in trouble. I felt really guilty about it.

The next day, I decided to be honest with my parents and I told them I had damaged the wall. My mum and my dad were happy that I had been honest with them, and I felt so relieved that I'd told the truth and that my brother was no longer in trouble.

As a big sister I often felt a responsibility to set a good example for my little brother. Sometimes I found that annoying because I think my parents let him get away with more things than me (they still do and he's twenty-nine!), but it also meant we were close and I loved how he looked up to me.

My favourite memory of Oliver was when he was about three years old, and he would wake up really early on a Saturday morning. Instead of going into our parents' bedroom he would always come and wake me up. I was never bothered because I always loved seeing him. He would climb into my bed and we would talk for hours until our parents woke up. I would also make up games for us to play so that he didn't get bored. Looking back, those are some of my favourite memories of growing up.

So, even if your brother or your sister drives you up the wall, you should never take them for granted. Appreciate them, because one day you might live very far away from them and won't be able to see them as much! Ollie, I miss you!

ROSIE'S ROUND-UP!

There's a saying:

'You can choose your friends, but you can't choose your family.'

No family is perfect and most will get on each other's nerves quite easily, but that's usually because you know each other incredibly well and care about them.

Whatever happens in your life, your family or friends will always be there for you. So remember to make time to be there for them – even if they drive you up the wall!

CHAPTER
TWELVE

SAYING
GOODBYE

PAIRING SNACK
Your favourite chocolate biscuit or a tasty cereal bar
Both great for dipping in warm drinks.

PAIRING DRINK
Some warm milk with honey
So soothing and delicious.

I SHOULD READ THIS WHEN . . .
I need to say goodbye to somebody I really care about.

ROSIE'S RAMBLINGS

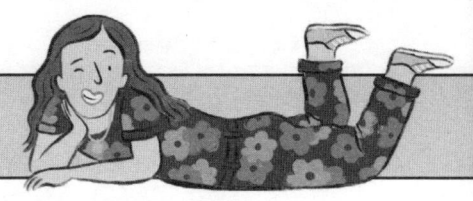

Saying goodbye can mean a million different things. It could be bye for just a little bit, like when school's done for the week or you're off on holiday, or it could be a more permanent goodbye when you know you'll never see that person again. But whether it's somebody leaving or somebody passing away, goodbyes are never easy.

I never like saying goodbye and if I had my own way, I would stay with people forever. I even get emotional when I get off a bus: 'So long, bus driver, you have driven us well.'

But saying farewell is a part of life that we all have to go through and learn to move on from, too. People leave our lives in all kinds of ways and other people join it. We can't stay on the same bus forever.

How did the bus driver say goodbye to the fish?
Catch you later!

Don't leave meeee!

You might need to say goodbye to somebody because they're moving to a different school, a different town or even a different country. If they're a good friend of yours, this might feel really difficult because you are used to seeing them every day.

It's okay to sometimes feel a little bit angry in this situation. I feel angry when one of my friends tells me that they're moving away. I sometimes want to ask them, *Don't you like me any more?* But I always remind myself that they are not leaving because of me – it's for another reason and most importantly, it's the best decision for them and their family.

I remember when my friend Tim moved to Australia a few years ago. I was gutted. I would no longer be able see him any time I wanted, and Australia is *so far away*. It's more than twenty-two hours away on a plane!

Before he left London, Tim had a big leaving party. We talked, we laughed and we hugged. I told him how much I loved him and how much I enjoyed being his friend.

When he moved, we were able to talk loads online and FaceTime whenever we missed each other. Even though he is literally on the other side of the world, he never feels too far away because we talk often.

Now, whenever I go to Australia for work, I visit Tim and it feels really special to see him. Even if we have gone literally years without seeing each other, we are always able to pick up where we left off and we still are the best of friends.

It might feel sad when a friend or somebody close to you leaves, but it doesn't mean you'll never see them again. There is always the internet and other ways you can keep in touch. You could even go proper old school and start writing letters to each other! And when you do meet up – however long it's been – you will have so much to catch up on. Plus, if you're close friends like Tim and I, it will feel as if you have never been away from each other. Friends forever!

Goodbye, I love you

And then there are the real goodbyes. The forever ones. The ones that have to happen when somebody dies.

Before I start this bit, I want to remind you I am only a comedian and all I can talk about is my experience of what it's like when somebody passes away. If you want real, proper advice because somebody close to you has died, there are so many clever and brilliant people who can help you much better than I can.

It's okay to speak to a doctor or a counsellor if you're struggling to cope with grief. Speak to your parents or caregiver and they can help you get the support you need.

The first person close to me to die was my grandpa. His name was Harvey Jones and he was brilliant. He was the best storyteller I knew and he would talk for hours and hours, telling us all about the people he knew and the

adventures he went on when he was younger. He was so clever and spoke so many languages, and he *loved* music, especially opera.

He was terrible at remembering names though, and when he saw you he would call you every other name in the family before getting to your name.

'Ah, hello, Rob, Andrea, Elena, Richard, Oliver, no, ROSIE, that's it, Rosie!'

He was eighty-two when he died and we knew it was going to happen because he had been ill for a while. He was okay about dying because he said he'd had a good and happy life. He had spent it drinking a lot of fine wine!

Even though we had time to say goodbye, it was still very sad when he passed. I couldn't believe I would never have another conversation with him again. I would've done anything for him to be there for one more day, even if he did forget my name again.

Now that I'm grown up, I still think the fact that people and our beloved pets have to die is the most annoying part of life. I wish we could all stay here, the same, with each other, forever. Wouldn't that be really lovely?

Unfortunately, life isn't fair and sometimes we need to say goodbye to a person we love sooner than we want to.

If you want to cry, cry.

If you want to scream, scream.

But if you can, remember the good times. Remember the times they made you laugh and remember how they made you feel. Remember the good days you had and remember how special they were to you.

They might not be here any more, but they are still in your memories and in your heart. Those will never fade.

Never forget the people you love

If you miss somebody you care about, simply think of all the great things about them and how much better your life is because you knew them.

Missing somebody can often feel like a negative emotion, but in a way it's a positive one. The fact you miss a person shows you care about them and love them.

At the moment, I am missing my friend Charlotte. She is my best friend from university, and when we were teenagers, we were inseparable. But recently, she has been living in Switzerland (which is really good for skiing), so I haven't been able to see or talk to her as much as I would like to. Here's a list of all the great things about Charlotte:

- **She is incredibly kind and thoughtful. I used to call her my 'second mum' because she used to cook for me when we were at university.**

- She is so artistic and can make a million different things. Dresses, cushions, curtains, moose heads – you name it, she's stitched it.

- She's so honest and I love it when she tells me I'm *not* being funny! This is always helpful when you make a living trying to make people laugh.

- I love how we are able to spend so many hours together talking about nothing. She knows me the best in the world.

- I love how we can totally be ourselves when we're together. She doesn't expect anything from me, and we love each other no matter what.

Charlotte, I love you, I miss you and I am so glad that we are friends.

Now, it's your turn! Think about a person or a pet you miss very much, then write down why you miss them and five great things about them.

ROSIE'S ROUND-UP!

Sometimes, if I am walking home
from the shop or lying in bed in the morning, I like to pick
a person in my life (usually a family member or a really
good friend), and think back to all the amazing things
we've done together.

I use my mind and my memories a little bit like a
scrapbook, where I stick down and piece together all the
memories I have with that person.

I'm a firm believer in living in the moment but sometimes
it's lovely to let yourself look back and see how far you've
come with that other person.

If the time comes when you need to say goodbye to
someone, it's important to hold on to your memories of
them. The memories will make it feel as if that person
has never left your side.

CHAPTER THIRTEEN

THE FUTURE AND BEYOND

PAIRING SNACK
Fruit with a bit of crunch like an apple

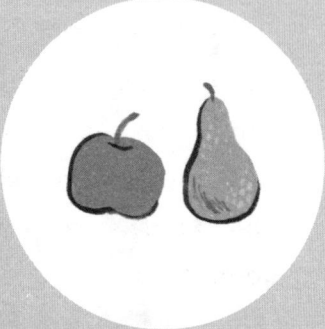

PAIRING DRINK
Posh lemonade – in a fancy glass if you have one!

I SHOULD READ THIS WHEN . . .
I am thinking about getting older and what my future will look like.

ROSIE'S RAMBLINGS

When I was at school, I had so many plans for the future. I was so ambitious and all I thought about was being a grown-up. I had planned my life so specifically that I thought I knew exactly what I wanted to do and who I was going to be.

> # I had decided to be a writer and live in London.

To be fair, I have done exactly that because here I am, writing this book in my flat in London!

But not *everything* has gone exactly how I imagined – I also wanted my own bakery and I haven't got that yet, have I? But you never know what's around the corner . . . hopefully doughnuts!

But some things have gone in a direction that I never would've imagined. If you could tell twelve-year-old Rosie that she would grow up to be a stand-up comedian, she would have laughed in your face – and not in a good way.

I had no idea that somebody like me could ever become a comedian because when I was younger there were no disabled comedians. I had no role models to look up to, so I had no idea that this was a career I could have.

Who is the old you?

- **What does getting older mean to you?**

- **Where do you think you'll be living?**

- **What job do you think you'll have?**

- **Who will your friends be?**

- **Are you excited about getting older?**

Think about it or write it down on a piece of paper.

For me, getting older included the ability to do what you want without worrying what other people think about you.

I also thought getting older meant that, at some point, I would become a serious adult – but I'm thirty-three years old and still burst out laughing whenever somebody farts! I don't think I am going to become a proper adult any time soon.

How do you know a clown has farted? It smells funny!

Basically, your future self is whoever you want to be. The world is your oyster and there's so much of it out there for you to explore.

Now, that sounds *seriously* exciting, doesn't it?

Never be afraid of change

I understand this sounds scary but change can be scary – especially if you are happy with where you are and what you are doing. But the thing about life is that it changes, all the time, and the only thing we can do is hold on for the ride and enjoy the adventure. Change can be really fun.

It sometimes feels like **EVERYTHING** is about to change and move on and you have no control, but that's the thing – you do!

It's *your* future; do what you want with it. Make noise, make a change in the world for the better and make sure to do something **FABULOUS**.

The biggest change I made is when I decided to leave my steady job to become a stand-up comedian. A lot of people in my life thought I was crazy. I had always made people laugh but never had I tried to make a career out of it.

Becoming a stand-up comedian felt scary because there were a lot of questions that I didn't know the answers to yet.

Was I really funny enough to be a proper, full-time comedian?

Will I ever be successful?

What will I do if nobody laughs at my jokes?

Will I be able to make money from comedy?

Am I making a HUGE mistake?

I couldn't answer any of these questions until I tried becoming a stand-up comedian. And I knew I would regret it if I didn't try.

That is a key thing to nailing the future . . . asking yourself, *Will I regret it if I don't try this?*

Another thing I ask myself when I'm not sure whether I should do something is, *What's the worst that could happen?* Usually, the answer is, *Not a lot.*

For example, if the worst thing happened and I ended up not being a very good comedian, I could've simply gone back to my old job, which I still really enjoyed. I could've sat at my desk and thought, *Oh well, the comedy thing didn't work out, now let's crack on with work.* But at least I wouldn't have sat there for years, never knowing whether I would be successful or not.

But, luckily for me, the stand-up comedy thing *did* work out – woo-hoo! Now I have my dream job where I can travel the world, write books and make people laugh. I really am living the dream.

If you ever have the opportunity to try something different, *do it*. What's the worst that could happen? If it doesn't quite go to plan at least you can say you tried it.

I always say that we only live once and that life is too short to live with what-ifs!

The future is tomorrow!

When I was at school, whenever we talked about the future it always felt like it was a million years away. But really, the future could be whatever you want it to be. The future is big and small all at the same time. You'll have some big decisions to make but it will take a lot of smaller steps to get there.

212

Sometimes I find the idea of the future overwhelming. I don't know how I will do everything I want to do. It'll be so hard to fit everything in.

So, when the future feels a bit much, narrow down your goals to just the week ahead or even the day ahead. This will make things much more manageable for you.

You could even try setting yourself one goal a year. This goal could be a really big one like saving up money for a game you want, or it could be really small like making sure you brush your teeth for two minutes every time.

My goal is to go on one holiday in the next year. My job is really fun but it can be very busy, and I often find it difficult to make time to rest. So next year I'm going to have a gorgeous holiday and do nothing but relax and have fun!

I love going on holidays, especially somewhere hot with a beach. I love lying down on a sunbed and doing nothing but reading my book for hours.

What's your goal for the year?

ROSIE'S ROUND-UP!

When I was at school, I would dream about graduating university and getting a real, adult job. I would spend hours daydreaming about the future. Who I would be, where I would live, what job I would do, who my friends would be. It was so fun to dream about it all!

Now that I'm grown up and doing all the things I dreamed about, all I want is to be young again. I don't think I properly appreciated school or even the town I lived in, until I left.

While it's good to think about the future, don't forget about right now. Being at school will create some of your best memories and you'll never get as much time to spend with your friends as you have now. It's great to think and plan for the future, but don't forget to live in the **NOW**.

THE BIG CRUNCH

Well done, you've made it to the end of my book – woo-hoo, go you!

I hope *Moving On Up* helped you beat the bullies, accept your differences and grow in confidence. I really hope that it continues to help you for many years to come.

Writing this book has been an incredibly special experience. It's allowed me to relive some lovely moments from my childhood and remember some eventful memories – even though not all of them were good (sorry for the Monopoly vom story on page 54 . . .).

Every part of growing up comes with its own set of strange changes and unique challenges, and sometimes you might wish you were small again – being small was easy, wasn't it!?

But getting older can also be brilliant, especially as you figure out who you want to be when you grow up.

It's really hard to sum up getting older and dealing with change, but here's my one tiny bit of advice for it all:

BE KIND.

That's it. Simple. Two small words.

Consider the feelings of the people around you and never hurt somebody just because you can.

There might be moments where you'll believe it'll make you feel better to hurt somebody who has been mean to you, but it *won't* help you feel better about yourself.

And, when in doubt, eat crisps. Crisps make everything better.

Why not try Rosie Jones's hilarious series
The Amazing Edie Eckhart!

If you liked this book, why not try ...

ACKNOWLEDGEMENTS

This book has become an accidental love letter to all of my friends – you know who you are. Thank you for being kind, patient when I don't reply to your messages, and the best company on a night out!

My family, as always, for being the most supportive bunch a gal could wish for. I love you soooooo much.

Flo, Lily, Kizzi, Katy and all of the Off The Kerb team. You go above and beyond what an agent should do. Thank you for making my dreams come true each and every day.

Thank you to Helen, Jen and the whole gang at Hachette for making my dreams of becoming an author into a reality. Your kindness, patience and unwavering support haven't gone unnoticed. You're wonderful.

Of course, a HUGE thanks to Hayley, the illustrator, for bringing this book to life. You have done an amazing job. It looks SO COOL!

And thank you to you, the reader, for getting to the very end of the book – you did it! I hope this book has helped you, or made you feel better about growing up. It's such an exciting time ... trust me!

Photo © Aemen Sukkar

ROSIE JONES is a comedian, actor and writer. She has fronted her own travelogue series called *Trip Hazard* on Channel 4 and can also be seen on countless hit television shows, including *Live At The Apollo*, *The Jonathan Ross Show*, *The Last Leg* and *Casualty*, to name a few!

In her spare time, Rosie loves seeing her friends, eating sausage rolls and Scotch eggs, listening to Taylor Swift and playing *Candy Crush*.